ACCESSING PARENTHOOD

STORIES BY AND ABOUT PARENTS WITH DISABILITIES

Edited by
Susie Angel & Laura Perna

OLEB
Books

OLEB
Books

333 Washington Ave. N.
STE 300-9029
Minneapolis, MN 55401
www.olebbooks.com

Copyright © 2024, Susie Angel and Laura Perna
All rights reserved.
No part of this publication may be reproduced, stored in, or introduced into a retrieval system, or transmitted, in any form or by any means (electronic, mechanical, photocopying, recording, or otherwise), without the prior permission of the publisher.

Requests for permission should be directed to
info@OlebBooks.com

Edited by: Susie Angel and Laura Perna
Assistant Editor: Belo Miguel Cipriani
Copyedited by: Ellen Morgan
Book Cover and Interior Design by: Monkey C Media
Author Photo Credit: Coalition of Texans with Disabilities

First Edition

Printed in the United States of America

ISBN: 978-1-7323127-8-4 (paperback)
ISBN: 978-1-7323127-9-1 (ebook)
ISBN: 979-8-9897474-0-5 (audiobook)

Library of Congress Control Number: 2024938101

For Susie

CONTENTS

Foreword / 1

Growing Up with Me and My Invisible Disability / 7
Wendy Kennar

Coloring Unicorns and Popping Wheelies / 17
Jennifer Heettner

Parenting After Stroke / 30
Delanie Stephenson

Little Stuffed Grape Leaf / 39
Lou Evlalia

Maybe: The Motherhood Thing / 54
Stella Carruthers

Don't Fall, Mister / 73
Reine Dugas

Hearing My Son's World / 84
Dylan Ward

Three Days Before the Witches Fly / 95
Suzanne Nielsen

It Must Be in Our Genes / 102
Kaz Morran

Acknowledgments / 119

About the Editors / 121

A Tribute to Susie / 123

FOREWORD

Neither Susie nor I ever thought we would be at the helm of an anthology, despite our backgrounds. Between the two of us, we had completed a journalism degree, an English major, storytelling projects in many forms, scholarly articles, and a LOT of reading. But we had never published anything, let alone a book that focused on the experiences of people with disabilities. Until...

In 2009, I began volunteering at the Coalition of Texans with Disabilities (CTD), a public policy nonprofit in Austin whose mission is to ensure that all Texans with disabilities can work, live, learn, play, and fully participate in the community of their choice. Much of my work revolved around the advocacy team's activities at the state capitol and grassroots organizing, but CTD's leadership has always encouraged passion projects that support its mission. So, when I pitched the idea of an annual statewide creative writing contest centered on disability, Executive Director Dennis Borel said to run with it. The Pen 2 Paper disability-focused creative writing contest launched in February of 2010. Texas writers of all abilities were invited to submit fiction, nonfiction, poetry, and comics that addressed the topic of disability in some way. Personal experiences, cultural criticism, family histories, fictional main characters with disabilities—nothing was off the table, and, having little idea what to expect, I was astonished and humbled at the response. That first year, we received 63 submissions from every corner of the state.

Pen 2 Paper 2010 was still taking submissions when Susie interviewed at CTD that summer. CTD offered her a position, and she took it, on the condition that she was allowed to enter the contest. This was no small thing—she was getting frustrated looking tirelessly for her first "real" job but found that no one would hire a woman with severe quadriplegic cerebral palsy. But she couldn't pass up the chance to enter the only contest she'd ever heard of that focused exclusively on disability experiences and perspectives.

After CTD hired Susie, she joined me to manage Pen 2 Paper as a co-coordinator, and the contest really took off. In the following decade, Pen 2 Paper would grow and evolve. Dozens of entries submitted each year turned into hundreds as we (at Susie's urging) opened the contest to international writers.

Each year, we received work on so many viewpoints surrounding disability, and we always learned something new. Authors sent in their screeds against ableism and their rallying cries to take pride in disability culture and community, accounts of fighting for their kids with disabilities in impossible public systems, struggles against overprotective (or worse) parents, the heartbreaks of Alzheimer's disease, dark journeys with mental illness that ended in triumph or defeat or had no real resolution at all, slices of every kind of life, science fiction stories, love stories, tributes to service animals, and so, so much more.

What writers from the world over shared with us about their own lives or from their imaginations was an incredible gift that still awes and humbles us both. You can read many of our winners and finalists at txdisabilities.org/pen-2-paper.

As Pen 2 Paper grew, it produced some offspring of its own—a monthly inclusive open mic, still going on virtually due to COVID, and this collection.

Our collaboration with Oleb Books began when founder Belo Cipriani heard about our work from a Pen 2 Paper–winning author. Belo saw his and Pen 2 Paper's goals as closely aligned and asked whether Susie and I were interested in serving as editors for Oleb Book's next anthology. Were we?! For years, we had been talking about doing an anthology to broaden the reach of the incredible work of Pen 2 Paper writers. After a couple false starts, it was clear we didn't have the capacity or enough knowledge about publishing to pull it off on our own.

Another important factor in our decision was that, from the beginning, Belo articulated his commitment to paying contributors to the anthology. By now, Susie and I had learned well that artists and authors with disabilities often found that they were expected to produce work for free. But "exposure" doesn't pay the cost of living, and Belo's prioritizing of artist compensation added to our enthusiasm of working with him.

Belo asked how we felt about a collection of stories on the theme of parenting and disability. This really struck a chord with us: in our lives, in the media, even in public policy, we encountered the laughably inaccurate notion that people with disabilities don't have personal experiences with sex, romantic relationships, or the decision to have a family. Even putting "parent" and "disability" in the same context felt gleefully transgressive. We took Belo up on his offer.

For Pen 2 Paper 2018, we added a division specifically for the anthology, the Oleb Books Personal Essay Award (OBPEA). As entries began to come in, we realized that there were so many different viewpoints to this theme. We received work by parents with disabilities, adult children of parents with disabilities, people with disabilities reflecting on how they were parented as children, and even adults with disabilities grappling with the decision to have children. You'll see all of these represented in the following pages.

The next year, we began working with the selected entrants on their pieces for the anthology. The editing process was a real learning experience. We sometimes gave feedback on Pen 2 Paper stories when authors asked for it and we had the time. But to work with an author on refining their own story was something else entirely. It was personal! And emotional! Our goal was to preserve every author's voice, but we also didn't want to hold back on making suggestions we thought would strengthen the delivery of their messages. We think we eventually struck the right balance, and we're grateful for the interactions we got to have with each of these authors.

The editing process for some of the entries continued into 2020 until the COVID-19 pandemic hammered the publishing industry. Suddenly, our production timeline and plans to release the anthology nearly came to a halt. On top of that, Susie's breast cancer metastasized twice to her brain. She underwent brain surgery, a month of rehab, and radiation treatments. It was hard on her. If she had dropped out of the project, no one would have faulted her. But she was determined to work with the authors and put the anthology together because it meant a lot to her.

So, we pushed our deadlines back again and again as weeks of uncertainty turned into months and, then, a few years. It's impossible to overemphasize how grateful we are to the authors in this collection for their unending patience as we delayed and regrouped, not only with progress on the book, but also their paychecks!

But the book did progress, and here we are.

As with Pen 2 Paper, the themes and tones you'll find in these nine stories don't represent a monolithic experience of disability or parenting.

Strongly running through many of them, though, is the fact that being disabled and being a parent, in real life, aren't two separate things. They become and inform each other, often in ways that wind up supporting the child.

Some stories articulate pride in the disabled body and mind, which authors uncovered, in part, in becoming parents: Suzanne Nielsen's multigenerational journey, "Three Days Before the Witches Fly"; Kaz Moran's globe-trotting adventures, "It Must Be in Our Genes"; and Lou Evlalia's hard-won self-discovery in "Little Stuffed Grape Leaf."

Wendy Kennar is much more matter-of-fact, navigating family activities in "Growing Up with Me and My Invisible Disability."

Doubt, anxiety, and uncertainty are the strong emotions in Delanie Stephenson's "Parenting After Stroke" and Dylan Ward's "Hearing My Son's World." In raising their children, both are overwhelmed by systems and a culture that aren't designed for people with cognitive or hearing impairments.

In "Maybe: The Motherhood Thing," Stella Carruthers describes how her own identity as a disabled woman is intertwined with the decision of whether to become a parent in the first place.

Elsewhere in *Accessing Parenthood*, authors tell stories about their own parents. In "Coloring Unicorns and Popping Wheelies," Jennifer Heettner reflects as an adult on how her parents communicated with her (and didn't) as a child about her mother's disability. Reine Dugas steps into a caretaker role for her father after an Alzheimer's diagnosis with "Don't Fall, Mister."

It's best to let these tales of adaptation, self-discovery, honesty, and giving and receiving unconditional love speak for themselves. Whether you are disabled or a parent yourself, it is our hope that you'll laugh, empathize, relate, learn, and celebrate these authors as you read their stories. Enjoy.

—Susie Angel and Laura Perna

GROWING UP WITH ME AND MY INVISIBLE DISABILITY

WENDY KENNAR

"How about horseback riding?" Ryan asked.

We were having dinner and brainstorming ideas for a fun family summer adventure, a tradition our family had started, inadvertently, seven years ago. And I wanted to keep the tradition going.

Our annual trips as a family began the summer before Ryan, then just four years old, started preschool. We took our first and only trip to Disneyland. We live in Los Angeles, so while Anaheim is a bit of a drive, we are still close enough to visit the self-proclaimed "Happiest Place on Earth" regularly. But we don't, because amusement parks are difficult for me to navigate. And, thankfully, Ryan's not a big fan of long lines and crowds, so he's never asked to return.

The following summer, we ventured further from home and drove up the coast to Cambria, where Ryan experienced his first hotel stay. Since then, we've tried to take yearly trips (either during spring break or summer) to the place I feel most at peace. And, thankfully, Ryan enjoys our low-key days of kite flying, beach sitting, and ocean watching as much as we do.

And now Ryan was about to enter middle school. A family trip wasn't possible this summer because of scheduling conflicts: my husband's retail schedule and Ryan's basketball camp schedule. So, this year's adventure needed to be something we could do in a day.

Ryan liked the idea of a hot air balloon ride (my dad and I had gone over twenty years ago and loved it), but my husband vetoed it. And deep down, I worried about my ability to climb in and out of the basket. As it was, there were nights when my pain was bad, when it felt as if I had invisible weights strapped around my legs. On those nights, I struggled to step in and out of our bathtub to take my shower.

Ryan and I talked about parasailing (I had done that over fifteen years ago), but my husband opposed the idea of his "two favorite people dangling in the sky, attached to a boat by a string." And again, I quietly worried that the physical stress would prove too much for my body. I remembered one adventure a few years ago, sitting next to Ryan on the Technic Coaster at Legoland, our hands clutched together, as we screamed our way through a fifty-foot drop. How would we handle being five hundred to eight hundred feet above land? I feared that my body would tense up, worried about my non-swimming son up above the open ocean.

Horseback riding was on the ground. It wasn't prohibitively expensive. It was nearby. My husband reluctantly agreed to it.

It was doable. Kind of.

Except maybe not for me.

I live with an invisible disability, an autoimmune disease called Undifferentiated Connective Tissue Disease (UCTD). When I was diagnosed more than ten years ago, my rheumatologist told me my illness was rare, that I could go ahead and call it "The Kennar" if I wanted, because most people would have never heard of UCTD. Truth be told, up until that point, I hadn't known what an autoimmune disease was. UCTD was a fancy way of saying that doctors didn't know exactly what was going on in my body, though they did acknowledge my illness shared overlapping symptoms with lupus, rheumatoid arthritis, and myositis, without my disease being any of those three more easily recognized, more easily understood disorders.

Daily, it means I live with pain, fatigue, and weakness in my legs, with my left leg being worse than my right. The hardest part, especially as a mother, is that my pain is often random, striking without rhyme or reason. Of course, there are certain activities I know will make me hurt. Wandering through the Natural History Museum for four hours is one of them. Going for a family bike ride is usually one of them. Bending, squatting, and stretching to tend to my garden is another one. But sitting is just as complicated. The seats at Crypto.com Arena are quite close together, and my legs feel squished when we go to cheer on our Los Angeles Clippers. I have had muscle cramps grip me until I'm crying, all while sitting on the couch with my son as we read a book together. And sitting in the car for hours on our beloved trips to Cambria is my least favorite part of the trip.

Sitting on a horse for an hour, my feet in stirrups, my legs in a fixed position, was most likely not going to be comfortable for me. I also wondered if I would even be able to swing my leg up and over to get on and off the horse. Beyond the event itself, I worried about lasting pain, the aftereffects, what I internally refer to as a "pain hangover."

But it was more than the actual horseback riding.

As much as I was worried about my own potential discomfort, I was just as worried about what my answer would mean to Ryan. What message would I be sending if I always erred on the side of caution and declined to ride a horse this time? Who's to say what form our fun family summer adventure would take three years from now, when Ryan would begin high school? If I agreed, made the plans, and went horseback riding, would I be demonstrating the valuable life skills of perseverance and resiliency? Was my let's-do-it-attitude fortitude or stubbornness or stupidity? Was my go-getter-ness a refusal to submit to my disease or a life-affirming decision to go out and do things that might seem scary, hard, and uncomfortable?

I didn't know.

I did know I wanted Ryan to grow up believing in himself and believing in the value of trying new things. Many things—food, music, places, experiences. Because they're new and different. Because he's curious. Because he wants to find out for himself.

I wanted Ryan to grow up living his life.

That's how I used to be. I went parasailing on Catalina Island. On another trip to Catalina, I went horseback riding. I went on a hot air balloon ride in Temecula. I explored San Francisco by myself, in the pre-smartphone days, relying on a paper map and my own common sense, intuition, and sense of direction, eating dim sum in Chinatown and a Nutella crepe in Haight-Ashbury. And even in my neighborhood, I often took myself out—to the movies, the local art museum, for coffee.

More and more now, as the years go by and I reluctantly acknowledge the truth—my autoimmune disease is not temporary—I regard every activity with an increasing level of apprehension, hesitation, and fear. Fear of the immediate pain. Fear of the pain that will follow. Fear that the pain I know now is just the tip of the iceberg, that I could do something to drastically worsen my illness. (Though doctors have never told me this is a possibility, and have in fact encouraged me to stay active, it is still a fear.)

But that's *my* pain. *My* fear.

When I received my diagnosis, my first questions concerned Ryan. I worried that I had somehow harmed our young son. I was experiencing pain in my legs. Our son was considered a "late walker," having not started walking until he was almost two years old. Was there a connection? My rheumatologist assured me that the two events were unrelated. My autoimmune disease wasn't hereditary.

I don't want my reluctance, my trepidation, to be, either.

Because while I'm also trying to teach my son that not everyone's hurts are visible, that there are many reasons for someone to walk slowly, for example, even if they "look fine," I'm also trying to teach him that no one thing defines a person. Much like I am not just Ryan's mommy, I am not just a patient with an autoimmune disease.

When Ryan was a little boy and asking questions about everything he saw, he asked me about the "blue spots." He meant the parking spots reserved for those possessing a disabled parking placard.

At the time, I told him those parking spots were closer to the entrance and reserved for people who had trouble walking. We talked about the image on the sign, the picture of a wheelchair.

For years, I didn't have a placard. I thought I didn't qualify. Even though the state of California approved my "retirement due to a disability" and I no longer worked as a public school teacher, I didn't think I was "disabled enough" for a placard. I truly didn't feel deserving. Surely there were others who needed it more than I did.

In my mind, people like my late grandmother qualified for disabled parking placards. Multiple strokes and rheumatoid arthritis had ravaged her body. She couldn't walk unassisted, she didn't drive, and she most often got around in her wheelchair.

But the time finally came for me to admit I needed a disabled parking placard. Though I walk unassisted and independently, I walk slowly and sometimes, most times, with a great deal of pain. I sometimes need a closer parking spot. Sometimes it's simply a matter of picking my battles, so I don't waste my energy navigating the San Diego Zoo's parking lot, but instead conserve my energy and use my legs to walk and explore the San Diego Zoo itself. (Though on a summer visit to the world-famous Zoo, I did reach a point where I surrendered to the pain, crying on a bench and trying to gather my strength before continuing.)

One day, my then-six-year-old son and I were on our back patio. He was dancing to the Sara Bareilles song "Brave," and I was sitting on our glider, admiring his spirit and his dance moves. When the song was done, and Ryan's performance was over, he asked me what it means to be brave.

"Bravery" is one of those words and concepts like "love"—you know it when you experience it, but articulating its meaning isn't always easy.

At the time, I told Ryan that being brave means there might be something that you thought was too hard or too scary or something that you just couldn't do, but if you're brave, you try to do it anyway.

These days, if I'm honest and not leaning toward my usual humble, dismissive self, I can acknowledge my own daily bravery.

Through my actions and my words, I am trying to teach Ryan the broader definitions of strength, perseverance, and bravery. And along those lines, I'm trying to teach by example broader definitions for disability, pain, and handicap.

It doesn't look the same for all people. There is no one-size-fits-all definition. And even with myself, all those words take different forms depending on the situation I find myself in.

Years ago, I was referred to physical therapy. Though I received an early discharge when the therapist determined physical therapy wouldn't help me, during our few sessions, the therapist strongly encouraged me to never fully give in to the pain, to never spend all day in bed. I laughed and told him it wasn't even an option.

I have a child at home. I will never fully give in to the pain.

However, I am in a constant struggle with myself. With not letting my disease dictate my life. With not limiting my experiences, my joy, my pleasure. And with not overdoing it.

So, I keep pushing. Ryan and I ride our bikes. We regularly visit museums, spending hours wandering the exhibition halls. We go for leisurely walks in our neighborhood.

One Saturday morning in July, my husband, son, and I set out for our horseback riding adventure. The three of us, and our guide, wandered through Griffith Park on slow, gentle horses. I surprised myself by getting onto my horse, Mac, without much discomfort. As we wandered up the trail, noticing the increase in quiet and the decrease in people, I felt a substantial increase in pain. My entire left leg hurt. I tried to shift around on the saddle, but there was only so much shifting I could do. We stopped for a family photo, and I thought of asking our guide if I could get off my horse for a moment, just to stretch my legs. But I didn't. Because I knew once I got off, I wouldn't want to get back on. And I was not going to do that to my son.

Ryan hadn't stopped smiling. He loved his horse, Star. He loved the ride. He loved learning how to pull on the reins to make Star turn away from the branches he was trying to eat.

As we headed back, the pain intensified. I bit my lip. I clutched the reins tighter, until I felt my fingernails press into my palms. Still my leg throbbed. Back at the stables, I waited for my turn to dismount. I stood, and felt my knee slightly buckle, felt myself ready to collapse, and I grabbed on to a nearby pole.

I would not do this to my son.

I smiled. We returned our helmets, thanked our guide, and tipped him. We walked back to our car, washed our hands, drank water, and prepared to drive home.

The whole ride home, Ryan smiled and talked and chattered. "That was awesome!" "It was so peaceful!" "I loved being up so high!" "Did you see how I made Star turn?"

Yes. I had seen it. And thankfully, Ryan hadn't seen the tears that I fought back.

Later in the day, we talked about our sore bottoms. Finally, hours after our ride, my husband asked me how I felt. I looked at him and said, "I really hurt. But Ryan loved it."

That's what it came down to for me.

Ryan's bottom remained sore for about a day. My husband was sore for about a day and a half. I was sore, aching, in intense pain for days. All my usual tasks felt much more difficult. I grimaced as I bent to empty the dishwasher and return our clean dinner plates to their rightful spot in the cupboard. I gingerly hoisted myself up from our dining table, using both hands as leverage. I awkwardly contorted my body in and out of the driver's seat of our car.

A friend of mine, a woman who lives with fibromyalgia, applauded my decision to go horseback riding.

"At least your pain is from doing, as opposed to just being," she texted me after I informed her of our fun family adventure and my terrible distress and agony.

Another friend, a woman who has known me for over twenty years, a woman who can walk for over an hour and feel fine, chastised me—from the moment she learned of my decision to the email I wrote her telling her we had done it.

"Why do you keep doing these things, woman? You do it to yourself. What do you expect?" were her unsympathetic words.

Both of my friends were right.

A few nights after our horseback riding adventure, my husband was working late, and Ryan and I were having dinner together.

"Can we go horseback riding again?" Ryan eagerly asked.

In my head, the answer was a definitive "No way!"

At the table, though, I took a sip of water before responding to Ryan's question.

"I think horseback riding is a once-in-a-while adventure. It's not something we can do all the time."

"Because it's too expensive?" Ryan asked.

I looked at my son and knew I needed to say it. To be honest. The price *was* too much, in a sense.

"Not because of the price. Because being up on the horse was hard on my legs."

"Did it make you hurt a lot?" Ryan asked.

I smiled ruefully. "Yes."

"I'm sorry," he said. He turned his head away from me.

"Don't be. I'm glad we went. It was an incredible experience. We all had fun, right?"

Ryan nodded.

"It's just that certain things are harder for me to do. Certain things I can't do as often or as much as I'd like. Horseback riding is one of them."

I continued. "I'm not saying we'll never go horseback riding again. I'm just saying we're not going again this summer. I'm so glad we went and had this super special experience."

"Me too," Ryan replied.

"And see," I went on. "We know I can do it. We know it'll hurt. But we know I can do it. That's the most important thing. The pain fades. But we wanted a fun family summer adventure, and we had one."

Ryan is now almost fourteen years old, and I admit I'm not parenting the way I had thought I would. I don't always insist on Ryan eating the dinner I have made for my husband and myself and will make Ryan his own dinner instead. I let Ryan watch movies on his iPod touch during breakfast while I read the newspaper.

I also hadn't anticipated having conversations with my son about autoimmune diseases and how prescription medication shouldn't be shared between family members even though we share water bottles. I hadn't expected to "earn" a disabled parking placard before my seventy-three-year-old dad and seventy-four-year old mom.

But that's what happens when you have a child. Plans are often just suggestions. Whether you have a disability or not.

Maybe I hadn't planned on being a mother with an invisible disability, but it doesn't change the way I love my son. Maybe I am teaching my son lessons I hadn't expected to teach him. Maybe Ryan's levels of patience, empathy, and sensitivity have grown exponentially while he's growing up with me and my invisible disability.

There's a quote I like by Samuel Johnson that says, "Great works are performed not by strength but by perseverance."

I can think of no greater work, no greater honor, than raising my son.

COLORING UNICORNS AND POPPING WHEELIES

JENNIFER HEETTNER

"Why is Mommy in a wheelchair?" I asked my parents, who were lounging in the living room, my dad on the couch and my mom resting in her recliner, her new wheelchair parked next to her. I had been laying on the itchy shag carpet in my favorite bright-striped, terry cloth tank top, coloring with my prized Crayola box of sixty-four. As I noticed the spokes that felt inches from my face, I could smell the rubber from the wheelchair's new tires.

It was late August, and our suburban Long Island neighborhood was so thick with humidity that the only way to keep cool outside was to swim in a pool or at the beach. We didn't have a pool, but our living room was air-conditioned, so we stayed inside.

Everything went silent. Even the air conditioner rattle disappeared. I felt my parents' eyes on me, and I looked away. As I sheepishly looked back, Daddy sat up and smoothed the legs of his jeans against his thighs. I couldn't tell if he was angry. He lit a cigarette and dropped his Zippo lighter back onto the table with a sigh. It clunked hard against the wood. I felt bad, like I had done something wrong.

"She fell into a manhole," he said, running his fingers through his soft, white-blond wavy hair. He continued smoking his cigarette, knocking ashes into the ashtray on the coffee table. Mommy looked confused, and I had no idea what a manhole was.

"Huh," I exclaimed, still uncertain what Daddy meant, as I got up and wandered over to the bookcase, trying to avoid my parents' uncomfortable gaze. I loved running my hands against the smooth leather bindings of the *Encyclopedia Britannica* that lined the bottom two shelves, which were perfectly at my height. I looked down at the brown and white shag carpet and spun myself halfway around the metal pole that supported the wall-length bookcase.

"She fell into a manhole." This time he said it more authoritatively. He crushed out his cigarette. "You know those things outside on the sidewalk. The metal ones. Where the men climb down to fix things," he explained.

"Yeah." I still didn't quite understand.

"Well, they were fixing one once and didn't close it right. Mommy fell in and got hurt. Now she uses this wheelchair."

"Oh, okay," I replied. I still had no idea what he was talking about, but I didn't know what else to ask, so I just nodded and shrugged.

I stared at the wheelchair. It was so ugly. Blue vinyl back and seat slung between metal frames. Big wheels with seemingly infinite fine chrome spokes that wanted to grab and chew little fingers that got too close. Hard rubber tires destined to run over little toes. An old-fashioned Everest and Jennings medical supply–issue wheelchair, the E and J sticker peeling on the side. When she used the wheelchair, my mother's slim, five-foot-four body seemed as if it was being swallowed whole by the chair. I just kept looking at the wheelchair. But it was like I could only look at it or at her; the two together did not fit. She was still my healthy, normal mommy. I didn't understand this new seating arrangement that came with us everywhere we went.

From the moment the wheelchair arrived, it was just suddenly part of everything. This cold, clunky metal thing in my face, in my way, banging into doorways, shoving its way into rooms in which it didn't belong. Mommy would try to maneuver it and end up stuck in weird places. And she hated it. She would get mad and bang on the wheelchair's arms, like she was trying to beat it up.

"This fucking thing," she would always say. "How did I get here?"

If she wasn't in the wheelchair, she was on the couch or in bed, maybe in the big, deep, brown velour armchair. I liked when she sat in that chair; it rocked and spun, and I could crawl up on her lap when she sat in it. The armchair was a good size for the two of us. She would rub my head and rock me to sleep in it. But she didn't really sit there anymore because it was hard for Daddy to get her out of it. She couldn't do it herself anymore. Right now, she was in the other, less deep and comfy armchair. She was reading too, her wheelchair parked beside her.

I used to be able to touch Mommy, to climb on her at will. Now I had to be careful so I didn't hurt her. But I didn't know how; she was suddenly breakable. I feared I would make it worse. The skin on her legs was so sensitive now. The wrong touch would cause her legs to spasm and kick, completely outside of her control.

But just like that, my mommy was now in a wheelchair. She was just "in" it. Suddenly it was hers, and she belonged to it.

Mommy fell in a hole and got hurt. This seemed reasonable enough, which I guess Daddy was counting on. My parents both seemed to sink back into what they had been doing before. And the wheelchair didn't seem so scary anymore. I walked over to it and ran my finger over the wheel. Mommy sat in one of the other armchairs, her wheelchair empty.

I laid back down on the itchy shag carpet and returned to my coloring book. I had just mastered coloring inside the lines and graduated to the big box of crayons, so coloring had become much more satisfying. And at that moment, I was more concerned about the unicorn in my coloring book that just had to be Crayola cornflower blue. I still didn't really understand anything more than before, but there was an answer, and it was something I could tell the other kids when they asked.

"You can sit in the wheelchair if you want," Mommy offered. Now Daddy looked surprised.

"Really?" I asked, unsure what to do.

"Sure, go ahead. Check it out."

Daddy looked at Mommy as though the wheelchair might be dangerous.

"Don't worry, Barry. The brakes are on. It won't go anywhere." Daddy nodded. I got up and clambered up into the wheelchair.

"See those little gray things on the side, try to move them." Mommy was showing me how to take the brakes off. "Try to push yourself," she said, smiling. I tried. It was hard to make the wheelchair move. I could barely reach over the arms, but it moved a little. I felt like I could get better at this. The wheelchair was way less scary.

Looking back as an adult, I realize now that this was the moment when we all made a pact. We might as well have pinky swore on the whole matter. This was our story, and we were now committed, like atheist parents perpetuating Santa so as not to destroy their child's innocence, the child unwittingly playing along. There was an unspoken promise that this would be our internal family narrative for as long as we could manage it. This was how they could protect their little girl from the roller coaster of disability that was just starting to unfold around them. It would take thirty-one years for me to understand and forgive this transgression.

Summer ended, and it was time to enter kindergarten. I was going to a new, fancy private school, along with my best friend Jessica. It was supposed to be a good thing: more attention from teachers because the school was small, and Jessica would be there with me. But the thirty minutes on the school bus felt like it took forever, and she wasn't on the same bus. Without Jessica, I felt alone and scared.

When it came time to leave for school in the morning, I kicked and threw myself to the ground, wailing and shrieking so my parents wouldn't make me get on the bus. My tantrums were otherworldly; I flailed, gnashing my teeth and throwing my body around, trying to physically show what I could not explain in words. No one and nothing could hold me, sobbing, raging, kicking. Unable to breathe, the guttural hiccupping cries of a desperate and inconsolable child. In those moments, there was only terror: heart racing, feeling trapped, pushed around by adults, unclear and unsure why my mother was hurt and broken and why they kept making me leave her in this state. I had no language, no way of understanding what was happening to me or in my brain.

Finally, deciding that getting me on the bus was too onerous, my parents started driving me to school, but I would resort to tantrums again as we pulled into the circular driveway of the ivy-covered brick building because I knew it meant it was time to be separated from my mother. Wailing from the backseat, I would hold on to the car door with all my might, kicking the seats as my father tried to pull me from the car. I just wanted to stay with Mommy. What if more bad things happened to her while we were apart? I didn't really understand the manhole explanation and so would envision her falling, falling everywhere, and getting more and more hurt.

We moved closer to school, and my teachers tried so hard to help me. Ms. Shattman, my kindergarten teacher, in her pink jumpsuit and her fun ponytails, would try to get me to sign contracts, to bring me out of the car and inside school with hugs and promises of sitting next to her when we were singing in the circle while she played guitar, and it slowly started to work. I managed to find my way through kindergarten and first grade, and school became more bearable.

As I got older, I also started to turn this whole manhole explanation over and over in my head. There was a major story in the news the summer I was eight, when little baby Jessica McClure fell into a well in Texas. It was on the news every day. They were drilling and waiting, trying to excavate around the well, and everyone was so scared she would die, yet she came out with only a broken leg. When I watched my mother try to get up to go to the bathroom and fall to the floor, her legs uncooperative and unwilling to support her; when I watched her struggle through transferring into and out of her wheelchair; when I watched as her muscle spasms caused her legs to go straight and rigid, so much so that she almost shot out of that wheelchair, I would wonder, could falling in a hole make all this happen? I had never seen the inside of a manhole, but falling straight down a big hole didn't seem like it could do all this.

The summer before my ninth birthday, my mom was at Burke Rehabilitation Center, an in-patient rehab far from our home. One beautiful summer Saturday, Daddy and I set out for the two-hour drive from Long Island to Westchester to visit her. I stared out the car window as the scenery changed from pretty houses with kids playing on front lawns to a major road with six lanes, strip malls, and fast-food restaurants. I really wanted McDonald's, but he always said no because we would have lunch with Mommy at Burke. I didn't know why it mattered since McDonald's was better to me and came with toys, but I knew from his tone that it wasn't an option. We got on the highway, and Daddy turned up the radio.

He belted out "American Pie" by Don McLean, and I followed along. This was our routine. Daddy loved singing it out loud when it came on the radio, so by now I knew all the words too. We approached the George Washington Bridge. I loved the height and the views of New York City. Maybe someday I would live in one of those apartments, high above the world, looking out from what looked like the drawer of a massive card catalog like at the school library, tucked away from the noise and busyness down below. I had been to the city with my parents to see the Rockettes at Christmas, and their stories about living there made it somewhere that I just knew was cool. Because I was nine, I was certain I knew what cool was. Daddy looked out at the city too.

"God, I loved living there. We had our first apartment on 23rd Street, near Gramercy Park."

This meant nothing to me. I wasn't even sure what to ask, but he answered, "It was such a great apartment—hardwood floors, high ceilings. We never should have moved out of the city," he said softly and wistfully smiled. He looked sad.

"I remember when I met your mother. We used to meet after work, and she would show up in these tall brown boots and this skirt to her knees with her silk blouses and short, dirty blond hair. She looked so put together! She used to strut her stuff."

"Eww, Daddy! Gross."

"Ah, c'mon. I was in love with your mother as soon as I met her. She was so funny and super smart. She used to run circles around the men she worked with, you know that, right?" I had no idea about this version of my mother, but I really liked hearing about her. And Daddy was smiling.

We got off the highway onto winding roads, with huge trees and woods. Before that summer, I had never been anywhere like this. It felt like we were in the country, like some faraway woods where fairytales might happen, like Alice in Wonderland was just behind the trees and shrubs. Daddy rolled down his window and lit a cigarette. He'd slung his tan left arm out the window, enjoying the drive. His cigarette smoke blew past, trailing behind us, and the fresh, crisp air wafted in. It felt cooler and shadier than it could ever be at home. I loved going. It felt far away and like an adventure with just me and my father.

Burke was a big campus, green and lush, with beautiful old buildings and high-tech rehabilitation facilities. It was a place where people were healing, getting stronger, getting back to their lives. At the time, I wouldn't have known how to describe it, but for once, my family felt optimistic. And I think it made Daddy happy to get to visit Mommy when she was acting more independent and like her "old self" and she didn't need him to lift her or move her from one chair to another. We would see her working out on interesting machines and doing impressive physical therapy and then have lunch. Sometimes she even walked in the parallel bars. Daddy loved watching her walk. My mother was only forty-one years old, and there were other young, and even younger, people at Burke. She didn't seem sick or hurt. She seemed like she was getting better.

Coloring Unicorns and Popping Wheelies

That was the summer we met Monica. She must have been in her mid-twenties. I would learn later that she had a spinal cord injury, and my father would explain to me how spinal cord injuries worked. But that detail didn't mean much at the time. All that mattered to me was that she was fun and hip and had beautiful hair that was always silky and kind of perfect. My frizzy curls would never look like that. And Monica was very agile. She would show me how to pop wheelies in her sporty wheelchair. I liked improving my wheelchair game. It felt like something only I, among my friends, could get "good" at. My mom was getting a sporty wheelchair like Monica's; that was part of why she was at Burke. Monica made me believe my mom could be strong, healthy, and fun—even if she did use a wheelchair.

We sat in the cafeteria. Neon posters with graffiti font lined the walls with inspirational sayings like "Don't give up, you got this!" and "No pain, no gain." Van Halen's song "Jump" played enthusiastically in the background. I fit right in among the 1980s decor and bright colors: my permed hair was up in a hot pink scrunchie, my hot pink leg warmers bunched around my ankles above my white canvas Keds, and my tie-dyed t-shirt, tied in a knot on one hip, hung down to my knees over my shiny blue leggings. I picked out this outfit myself, hoping Mommy would be impressed. I thought I was so cool.

Monica, her horse's mane of silky chestnut hair falling around her shoulders, sat relaxed in her Quickie wheelchair, elbows resting on her knees, a green ribbed tank top emblazoned with "Turk 182" on it showing her tanned, cut biceps and shoulders. She was strong and fit.

"I'm hungry. Let's go check out what's on for lunch. Your mom should be back any minute. We were just finishing up a class on transferring in and out of our chairs. She won't care if we get started on food." Monica flipped the brakes off her chair and spun around.

"I'll stay here and save the table," my dad said, perfectly happy to let me hang out with Monica. He knew I thought she was the coolest.

She maneuvered her chair like a professional skier or cyclist, someone we watched in the Olympics. Her chair was a piece of equipment elegantly in her control, enabling her to move through the world. She popped a wheelie as we made our way up to the counter. She was totally showing off, and I loved it. When I got distracted by the hues, hum, and flicker of the soda machine and began to struggle to use it, she wheeled over to my rescue, easily balancing her tray on her lap as she helped me pour an Orange Slice.

My mom rolled into the room. She was different. This was the first time I saw her in her new Quickie chair. It was sleek, black, and small and didn't swallow her whole. It had a low back, which meant my mom sat upright and tall. Skinnier, knobby tires gave her traction on the rubber floors. She rolled up to the table where my dad was sitting and spun herself around with a big smile, like a little girl spinning around in a new party dress. She was wearing makeup and a gauzy summer sweatshirt pushed up to her forearms. She was tan too. Evidently, she and Monica hung out outside when we weren't visiting. I pictured them smoking cigarettes and popping wheelies on the basketball court outside the big plate glass windows of the cafeteria.

Monica and I made our way back to the table.

"What, you started without me?" Mommy joked, eyeing our trays.

"Don't worry, hot stuff, I waited for you." Daddy smoothed it over. I guess Daddy was flirting with her, and she laughed out loud. I didn't get it, but I also didn't care. Flanked by Monica and my mom, I hopped up into one of the red, molded plastic cafeteria chairs. My dad got up and went to push my mom's chair so they could go up to the cafeteria counter together. She pulled on one wheel in a way that made her chair cut hard to the right, so he just missed the handles behind her.

"Oh, hey." He jumped back a bit, smiling. His assistance was happily admonished.

"I got it." She smiled and laughed as they started to make their way to the food line. As she caught some momentum, one hand shot up, and she ran her fingers through her short, frosted hair. It flopped back down on her face. She was beautiful, cool, and totally in control.

Later that summer, Mommy came home. She had a new sporty wheelchair, good energy, and biceps. We had moved to a new house earlier that year, and that summer they installed a lift for her wheelchair so she could get in and out independently. She was working on her wheelies, or at least showing me how to do them in her chair when she wasn't using it. But the grab bars in the bathroom weren't enough, and the sporty new wheelchair still didn't stop the spasms and weakness. She continued to fall. Continued to struggle. Continued to get weaker. Sometimes she would fall when it was just the two of us alone in the house. I was trained to call 911 or press the emergency button on the "I've fallen and can't get up" alarm. But Angelo, her physical therapist, would come and do therapy with her on the living room floor. She was trying to keep up the strength she had built at Burke.

Other things to accommodate her chair would soon appear: wheelchair lifts to deal with the steps and then a ramp for the new house with a stoop, a cargo box for the top of the car for storing a wheelchair, a converted van with hydraulic lift and hand controls so she could take driving lessons (though she never drove) but meant my father didn't have to lift her in and out of the car, countless medical devices, hoya lifts, grab bars—a veritable Service Merchandise catalog of medical equipment large and small—all experiments that would fail over time.

In the years since they had told me the manhole story, I had been turning over the specifics of falling into a manhole and getting injured. And, having now developed my vague understanding of spinal cord injuries, thanks to Monica, I struggled to understand how falling into a hole would cause all these ongoing problems my mother was having.

I don't remember the details of the day I asked. I think it was autumn because my dad was wearing his favorite checked shirt. We were in the kitchen, my dad at the head of the kitchen table, smoking a cigarette and reading the paper. My mom was at the counter cutting vegetables, despite the hard reach from her chair.

The memory is hazy. It was the first time I had ever confronted my parents. That day, I simply stood in our kitchen doorway, my ten-year-old hands on my ten-year-old hips, and asked my parents, "If Mommy fell into a manhole, wouldn't she have just broken something, even her back like Monica, and been able to start healing? Why is she getting worse? You can't get worse from an accident."

I didn't plan it. The time had just come.

"What?" My mother used her right hand to spin her chair ninety degrees. She stared at me, maybe glared at me. I was breaking the pact. I was demanding answers. It just didn't make sense, and my friends at school kept asking me more and more questions about what was wrong with my mom. I needed answers. Something didn't fit.

They both looked at me, startled, confused. I would like to imagine that they were at once strangely impressed by my young, curious mind's ability to refine my questions and call their bluff, horrified that the question had come so soon. They had no plan, only an inquisitive child with an endless stream of "Why, why, why?" They were left to confront the complex question that required a simplified explanation, accessible to a ten-year-old brain.

They looked at one another and, I would like to believe, gave each other some sign, some agreed upon "it's time to let her in on reality." They became matter-of-fact, I presume holding it together for their child, who couldn't possibly understand the gravity of what they were about to say.

My father's face was soft, maybe resigned, I'll never know. Like he knew that in the next breath, he would be giving me information that would change my life forever. Even though telling me would not be the thing to make it true, I can imagine that it felt like it might.

"Your mother didn't fall in a manhole. She has a disease. It's called multiple sclerosis. But people call it MS for short."

PARENTING AFTER STROKE

DELANIE STEPHENSON

On June 6, 2012, I suffered a massive brainstem stroke. Luckily, my husband, Curtis, got me to the hospital in time to receive a clot-busting drug called tPA, which did its job. Unfortunately, the medication that saved my life also caused hemorrhaging on the other side of my brain. The excessive bleeding along with the clot led me to be locked in. This meant I could only move my eyes. Nothing else would move. I also lost my ability to speak. I wasn't expected to survive the night. Doctors said if I did, I might never walk, talk, or swallow properly again.

My family was devastated. I had been happily married to my husband Curtis for eleven years and had two children: a girl, Katie, who was six, and a boy, Alex, who was four. My kids had witnessed me having the stroke, and I was terrified of how it would affect them. The last memory I had of Katie and Alex before entering the hospital was looking at them and wanting to call out "I love you." I opened my mouth, but nothing came out. Was this the last memory they would have of their mom?

I survived the first night, then the second, and spent several days in the ICU. When I was finally strong enough for therapy, the next step was a subacute hospital where I learned to speak, walk, and swallow foods again. The first word I whispered when

I found my voice was "home," the place where I longed to be. Next was "babe"—what I called my husband—then "Katie" and "Alex." My family was the most important thing in my life. I visualized playing with Katie and Alex and tucking them in at night. I wanted to hold hands with Curtis on the couch while watching TV. These visions were what filled my dreams at night. I was given an MP3 player and some relaxation recordings to clear my mind for sleep. I remember the voice on the recording telling me to close my eyes and imagine my happy place. Every night, I envisioned myself sitting in the front yard in my blue beach chair as my husband worked in the yard and my kids ran around outside, laughing. I didn't imagine some tropical island getaway. I just wanted to go home.

All along, my goal was to be discharged before Katie and Alex started school in the fall. My daughter was going into first grade, and my son was starting kindergarten. I wanted to see my son get on the bus for the first time. I wanted to be there when they got home and ask them how their first day was. I worked so hard in physical, occupational, and speech therapy keeping my goal in mind. Each step, literally, got me closer to going home.

When I was in the subacute hospital, Curtis came to see me daily, and my kids came once a week. I loved watching them play outside in the hospital garden. It was a little different than I imagined because I was in a wheelchair and they couldn't understand my speech, but anything was better than not seeing them. I cherished these times with my family.

While I was gone during the summer of 2012, I was so afraid Katie and Alex would forget who I was. During the twelve weeks I was in different hospitals, they were being sent from one relative to another while Curtis was still working to keep our insurance. My children's surroundings were constantly changing. Alex, who was fully potty-trained before the stroke, started regressing. I was so worried about that because of school starting. Katie had recently been diagnosed with ADHD, and I knew she was a handful. They both took medication daily and had doctor's appointments I was afraid they would miss.

Don't get me wrong. Everyone who stepped in to take care of them was great, but I was Mom. I had always handled everything dealing with my kids, and to not be in control was frightening. To not know what was going on with my family was horrible. I never knew for sure where Katie and Alex were or what they were doing day to day. Plus, I knew that the emotional problems they were having were due to being shuffled around from household to household. Everyone had their own set of rules, and none were what my kids were used to with me. I hated knowing there was nothing I could do.

When my kids came to visit me in the hospital and misbehaved, I automatically felt like I should correct them. I remember one time out in the hospital garden, Katie and Alex were running through the plants, and I said "stop." I don't know if they couldn't hear or understand me, but they kept running. They were being typical kids, but I wanted to show them I was still the authority figure. Their grandma, who was there, also told them to stop, and immediately, they listened. This tore me up inside. I started crying, and my husband couldn't figure out what was wrong. My nightmare was coming true: they wouldn't listen to me, but they would listen to someone else. I felt like my role as Mom was disappearing.

After six weeks of subacute therapy came two weeks of in-patient therapy. That August, I finally received news of my discharge date, and I was so excited. It was a week before Katie and Alex started school. I imagined coming home to a big celebration with family and friends and envisioned nightly routines of homework and packing lunches. Evenings filled with showers and picking out clothes for the next day. I would make up for lost time and be the mom they had missed all summer.

Dreams and reality are on two opposite ends of the spectrum, unfortunately. The day I was discharged from the hospital, I came home using a walker. Katie and Alex were happy to see me for about five minutes before running off to play. I spent my first afternoon watching TV and napping in a recliner. Not exactly the glorious homecoming I had imagined. I tried to hide my disappointment.

I couldn't help the kids shower and brush their teeth that first night. I couldn't tuck them in. They came to give me a hug and then were off to bed. Alex came back in the room a little while later and asked if he could stay with me for five more minutes. Curtis told him to go on to bed. I wanted to let Alex stay up, since I had been away from him all summer. What was five more minutes of cuddles after all I had missed? Curtis, however, strongly disagreed and made Alex go to bed. Curtis saw it as my son just weaseling his way into staying up later. I was furious and upset. I started crying. My heart hurt. It was then that I realized that coming home wasn't going to be as simple as I thought.

September came. On the first day of school that year, I was not able to see Katie and Alex get on the bus. This devastated me. I was at a day therapy program, and my mind was elsewhere at therapy that day. I wondered how my kids liked school, whether they made any new friends, what they had for lunch, and what their favorite subject was. I worried especially for Alex since kindergarten was such a big step, and he had just turned five. That evening, my kids didn't really talk about their day. They just wanted to play. I was tired from therapy (it seemed like I was always tired), so I stayed quiet and just sat in a recliner most of the evening. Curtis saw to it that Katie and Alex bathed and got ready for bed. My mother-in-law picked out their clothes for the next day. I sat in my recliner and watched, aching to be a part of it all. This was not at all what I had imagined.

As the school year progressed and fall turned into winter, we found a routine. During the day, I usually had therapy, Katie and Alex had school, and Curtis went to work. If I didn't have therapy, someone had to stay with me, usually my mother or mother-in-law. At night, I would try to read the kids a book, but my voice was usually tired at this point. I normally wouldn't last more than a few pages. Whoever was there to watch me that day would fix supper and help the kids with showers and bedtime routines. Again, I watched this all from afar. I just wanted to do normal mom things. I felt like it wasn't too much to ask.

My role as a mother had changed. I felt as if I no longer was the enforcer. I couldn't work, so I wasn't the provider. I could now hug, hold, and love on Katie and Alex, and they knew without any doubt I loved them. They loved me. But overall, I felt like an observer. I longed to feel needed. Mom couldn't get the kids something to drink, something to eat, or clean their room. Mom, who used to fold laundry and clean the kitchen, was in the recliner most of the time. Mom was to be taken care of, treated gently, and not bothered. But I *wanted* to be bothered. I wanted to help them with their homework, but even first-grade math was overwhelming. I wanted to fold the clothes, but after a couple of towels, I was exhausted.

The kids stopped asking me for things. They would go to Curtis or whichever grandparent was around. I wanted to talk to my husband about this, but he was tired from work and didn't really want to talk at night, or I was too tired from therapy to talk myself. The stroke that had physically affected me was taking an emotional toll on everyone else.

The first year after the stroke was tough. There was a lot of frustration and fighting between Curtis and me. We had to get used to these new roles that had been forced upon us, and it was hard to communicate at first. Plus, Katie and Alex, who had by then turned seven and five, were still in the needy stages, and we often focused on them when we should have focused on our marriage.

Another burden placed on Curtis was handling discipline. Before the stroke, it had not really been an issue. I could handle Katie and Alex fine in my husband's absence. Because I was a teacher, they were with me all summer long, and I loved to spend time with them. After the stroke, all that changed. Even the children's roles seemed to have altered. Katie became my nurse. Instead of me taking care of her, I felt like she was taking care of me. She would remind me to take my medicine, hold my hand in the parking lot and crowds, and pick up toys off the floor to make sure I wouldn't trip. Alex reacted to the stroke by becoming angry. He developed separation anxiety—he wanted to be always near me, but if something wrong happened, he blamed me. Everything was my fault. My sweet little boy started having awful temper tantrums and was getting physical with me. I couldn't handle him, and this hurt me to the core. What mother can't handle her own kids?

To make matters worse, doctors diagnosed me with pseudobulbar affect, also known as PBA, which meant that I would laugh or cry at completely inappropriate times. Every time Katie or Alex did something wrong, I would laugh like crazy, or if I was in a frustrating situation with my son especially, I would cry instead of getting angry when I should. It was awful. Curtis felt like he had to be the bad guy all the time, and while I wanted to show a united front, I often let the kids get away with things, knowing the whole time it was wrong. It made Alex's separation anxiety and anger issues get worse and exacerbated Katie's ADHD. It also caused friction between me and Curtis, who felt as if he now had three kids he had to take care of.

A year after the stroke, I finally felt like I could be alone with my kids during the day while Curtis worked. It was summer, and I usually had eight hours to fill. I could drive, and this helped get the kids out of the house. However, Alex's issues continued to go downhill, and as Katie got older, her ADHD seemed to get worse instead of better. This was what I called the summer from hell.

That summer, I dreaded watching my husband leave for work each day, never knowing when my meltdown was going to hit. I was usually in tears by the time Curtis came home. Weekends were my favorite times because my husband was home and could help with the kids. However, that meant I depended on him to be home most of the time, and he never had time to himself. We had many arguments over him not having an outlet, but did I? To make matters worse, I had fallen and broken my ankle, which Katie and Alex witnessed, and it traumatized my daughter—she never wanted me to go outside again. It just seemed like there was some type of catastrophe every day, and I was physically and mentally exhausted. I was relieved when school was back in session that fall.

Early in the school year, I got a call from the principal. Alex had been crying at school all day and couldn't be consoled. This quickly became a routine. I had to pick him up early almost every day. It got worse as time went on. Alex kicked a teacher's assistant. He was swearing at the principal. He was suspended. Play therapy and doctors and all kinds of testing became involved.

They sent him to another school. It embarrassed Katie to be the sister of the crying kid. A parent coach was brought in to show me ways to cope with everything. Curtis and I went to counseling, both individually and as a couple.

The next few years were a challenge. Doctors diagnosed my son with a seizure disorder. Several falls for me led to more hospital stays. Every time I had a new medical issue, Alex would react negatively, and it would freak Katie out when I got hurt. "We have to go to the hospital again!" she would cry. I thought I was seriously screwing up my kids.

After about two and a half years at his special school, Alex finally progressed enough to go back to his regular school. I wasn't falling as much. Katie was growing up into a beautiful young woman. My relationship with Curtis wasn't perfect, but we had learned to communicate in a way that worked for us. For a while, everything seemed smooth. We could do this. Our lives were way different from what we'd thought they would be, but life was doable.

Then puberty hit.

There are many books and experts out there that talk about how to deal with teenagers. The raging hormones, the interest in the opposite sex, the desire to fit in, the embarrassment to be seen with their parents, and so on. There aren't any books called *Parenting after Stroke, the Teenager Edition* (believe me, I've looked). Many of the pointers don't apply to a stroke survivor with PBA and other cognitive deficits who is the mother to a son with an intellectual disability and a daughter with ADHD, and the wife to a husband who feels like he's about to explode. We are not the cookie-cutter family. So, what works for some people will not work for us because of our limitations. We have been to several counselors, and no one has given us a concrete answer on how to handle two kids who love the heck out of me but do not respect me at all.

So, this is where we are. My son is now twelve, and my daughter is fourteen. Both are in middle school, and it scares me to death. This past year, things were so difficult that Curtis quit his job so he could be home to support me with Katie and Alex. I have a lot of guilt. We take things day by day. My husband tries to get me to look many years down the road to plan for things, and I just can't. Since the stroke, I must take it a minute at a time or I will have a panic or anxiety attack. Minute by minute is about all I can do.

Nevertheless, I am thankful for so many things. I am thankful to be here to spend time with my family, but this stroke has made it hard to be the parent I want to be. So much emphasis has been put on my health over the past seven years that I'm afraid Katie and Alex have become lost in the process. Doctors and therapists prepare you and your family for what to do in the event you fall when you go home after a stroke, but they don't tell you what to do when you feel like your family is falling apart. Strokes affect so much more than the person who has them. They affect anyone close to the stroke survivor, whether family or friends. I am not the same person I was before the stroke. I'm not better or worse. I'm just new. All I can do is my best in this journey called life, try to have some fun, and be the best mom I can be along the way.

My mom gave me the best advice a few years ago when things were getting rough with Katie and Alex. She said, "Just love them." That sounds so simple but so complex at the same time. But when it comes down to it, like the song says, "all we really need is love." So, I work hard every day to make sure Katie and Alex know that no matter how crazy it gets, Mommy loves them. If they know that, I'm sure everything will be okay.

LITTLE STUFFED GRAPE LEAF
LOU EVLALIA

My alarm vibrates. "Keep fucking going," the screen insists. Pain smothers me still. I'm always the last one to get up now, not rested, but ready to stop negotiating my head against the pillow. I've spent the night trying to avoid cervical subluxations, trying to keep my spine from partially dislocating and trying to keep pressure off my right occipital nerve. This morning, it is raining hard. I love the rain. It loves me back by affirming my desire to stay inside. A pulsing globe of pelvic pain kept me up for several hours last night. My legs were trying to run away from my body, regularly knocking my partner awake too.

I slowly and begrudgingly limp to the bathroom, drink some Cromolyn and take an old-fashioned antihistamine that a specialist prescribed, confusing all my local doctors, as usual. I started a new med yesterday too, and my body will have some extra surprises for me today, no doubt. It usually does, regardless. Iggy is already at school in their bedroom. They are in sixth grade this year and attending school fully remotely.

Iggy is a home-bodied and introverted child who has truly grown in confidence and self-awareness during quarantine. They got headaches and stomachaches daily, mostly from anxiety, when school was in-person before COVID-19. Those symptoms are rare now, though I still see my young self in their ongoing chronic leg and ankle aches. And I know they see their future in the way pain debilitates my body. I can't predict how or when disability will manifest in Iggy's future, but I'll continue crafting maps and devices of disabled wisdom to help carry them through.

I wasn't disabled when they were born. Or was I? My definitions have shifted so much through time. I know that I really did not like being pregnant. I was not straight, not a woman, and not out. Immediately after getting pregnant, I got strep throat with a 104-degree fever, and I told the doctor at my college clinic, after he very awkwardly congratulated me on my pregnancy, that I was planning on terminating, so it didn't matter what medications he gave me.

At the time, I was living in a dilapidated Victorian-style mansion with seven other students, a python, several ghost children in the attic, and a ghost cat that we all saw at least once. There was a claw-foot tub on the second floor that we never used, probably because no one ever cleaned the bathroom and it was disgusting. One night, in deep existential dread, I filled it with hot water and way too much lavender and submerged my whole body and head. My heart beat loud in my ears. Beneath the steady pounding was a tiny whisper, an impossibly distant second vibration. Looking back now, I know I must have imagined it, but somehow that was Iggy, in all their stubborn glory, demanding to exist. The next day I skipped my clinic appointment, against all of the evidence in my life, and imperfectly, irresponsibly, allowed my very stoned fate to take the wheel of my life.

I was twenty-one, majoring in dance and gender studies and working almost full-time. I had little respect for my own body or desires and was wading through years of unacknowledged trauma. For months my pelvis and ribs shifted painfully under my skin. I would roll over in bed and get stuck in a bad pelvic subluxation and need to be lifted into a sitting position to wait for the agonizing crunch back into place. There were days I couldn't breathe deeply or walk at all.

A friend told me once, as I lay despondently for weeks on the couch in our communal living room: "You're going to find a strength in you that you never knew you had." He didn't know me very well, but he was right. I went into debt with towing fees and parking tickets, trying to get my body and my Ford Escort as close to my classrooms as possible. I got gallstones and cured them with a twenty-four-hour fast of Epsom salt water finished off by a glass of pure grapefruit juice and olive oil.

The best thing about the person that got me pregnant was that his moms were witchy lesbian homebirth midwives. After finishing my thesis, I moved into the room above their garage/chicken coop with no running water in Bumfuck, Maine. Wabanaki land. Iggy came three weeks past their due date and, after three days and four nights of intense labor, was born into a Rubbermaid horse-feeding trough kept painstakingly warm by hauling pots of boiling water from the grandmothers' house next door. The first thing I said to their wide-eyed, purple, scrunched-up face was, "We're gonna be best friends."

I entered into parenthood reluctantly. For years I woke up in the morning surprised that it had happened. Iggy was determined to live, and I was terrified to break their tiny body. Postpartum depression flourished in my loneliness. Like many depressions, it told my brain that I should feel shame and forbade me to speak about it.

I waited for time to pass. I rocked in a chair for hours with a baby on my lap and read the entire *Lord of the Rings* trilogy. Vacations from reality have always been my best tactic for self-care.

I had to ease into my new life slowly. Having just left childhood myself, I was unprepared. My brother, who also became a parent by accident too young, told me to have a funeral for the life you thought you were going to have and then move on, so that you can be productive in this one. Despite the skepticism I have for my family's stealthy ability to breeze over genuine emotional thresholds in favor of practicality, that was solid advice.

* * *

The moment that began my journey toward identifying as disabled was my car accident at twenty-three. I was on my way to bartend at a wedding in the purple minivan my mom used to drive me to dance classes in. The backseats had been taken out to make room for five Styrofoam coolers holding three hundred lobsters. A man who had gone out to buy butter pulled out in front of me on a rural highway.

It was a head-on driver's-side collision. I refused ambulance transfer to the hospital and got picked up on the side of the road by a co-worker. I hauled kegs around with bruised arms all night. The pain in my right shoulder never went away after that. Months later, I had to sit down on the kitchen floor with the realization that I couldn't cut cheese off the block for Iggy's dinner anymore. I couldn't pick them up from bed to take them to the toilet for their late-night pee.

Every medical intervention just injured me more, until I had CRPS (an extremely painful, incurable, progressive nerve disorder) on the entire right side of my body and systemic throughout my central nervous system, with nearly every comorbidity. Turns out I'd also had an underlying hypermobility syndrome my whole life. Was it the Ehlers-Danlos that created the hospitable environment for multiple systemic chronic illnesses and pain? The unprocessed trauma? My closeted queerness and shame? The medical neglect and abuse? I truly do not know. Probably all of it. I won some kind of twisted acquired-disability bingo. At the time, I mourned that Iggy never got to know the person I thought was my true self, the dancer, rock climber, bike rider, power-tool wielder. I wanted to model that for them. I model something else now.

It took me the first two years of their life to get out of the relationship that had given me Iggy but taken so much. I used up every bit of the practiced repression I built in my lifetime until it broke me, literally. I couldn't deny who I was anymore; that couldn't be the message I raised my child with. Iggy deserved better.

The transition didn't go well. The year I figured out how to finally leave their father, Iggy got a case of whooping cough that has an impact on their lungs to this day. I had chronic panic attacks and severe rib subluxations. The apartment we moved out of had a bedbug infestation. Avalanches of guilt and blame pummeled me from every direction, including from inside my own head. Their father twisted reality to vilify me, most of all. I learned so much about how threatened people get by a mother who is perceived as not entirely self-sacrificing for their child, and by those who defy convention to live their own truth. I've also learned, over time, that being queer and disabled definitively makes me a better parent, and my only regret is how long it took me to truly embody myself as I am.

In order to live in my queerness and get out of a relationship with a deeply manipulative person, I had to give up partial custody of my child. It happened slowly. He would have them the mornings I worked, when I was working, then for one night, then two. Our agreements were so precarious. Their father would request more nights with them but leave them with his shifting girlfriends while he went out to smoke weed and play pinball. Iggy was three and being gaslit, but they noticed. When they came back to me, they would fall apart, and I became the place where they could depend on getting undivided attention.

It wasn't until Iggy was in third grade that, through an excruciating mediation process, my partner and I agreed on a fifty-fifty custody arrangement. I suppose everyone has a different experience with this. I search for scraps of gratitude that he wants to spend more time with Iggy and to be involved at all. Truly, though I know it's best for Iggy, I wish he didn't. I wish I could have my family and Iggy to myself. To never have to negotiate my parenting choices with someone who has broken my trust and Iggy's over and over. The custody arrangement negotiations, for me, were just another exercise in loss. As most of the things to which I had pinned my self-worth were dropping away beneath the weight of high-impact pain, I was losing hours and minutes with the most important person in my life. Iggy was a beautiful anchor of purpose and joy for me when life felt like it was becoming just a nightmare of constant pain. I've always been fiercely determined to make every decision in their best interest, and to do that, I've had to fight against some of the deepest pain in my heart.

I'm extremely lucky that I never had to go to court to negotiate the custody of my child. It is something their father and I both desperately wanted to avoid. I have always been afraid that he would leverage my disability against me to take Iggy away. That fear is still with me. For the first few years, I tried to hide my declining health. Internalized ableism told me lies about my self-worth every day, lies about myself as a parent that I'm still digging out.

The truth is that to become the parent my kid needed me to be, I had to slow way down. At first, I was too young to understand what that meant and would not have figured it out if I hadn't become disabled. I wasn't ready for my world to not be centered on me and what I wanted, but Iggy was old enough to show me, through tantrums and coughing fits, what they really needed. They didn't want to be brought to community organizing meetings several nights a week. They didn't want to be left with babysitters or even friends. They wanted to stay home and put on postmodern dance performances for me in our living room. They wanted all of my senses to be devoted to them and all of their magnificence. They needed to be shown that they were my highest priority, every day, as much as possible. I had to supply the presence and stability they were missing in their tiny life. Disability helped me shed the self-centered expectations I had about being able to do it all. I could do a little, and the most important thing I could do was giving presence and love to my child. Disability, ultimately, taught me how to become a parent.

In the middle of these massive upheavals in my young life, I fell in love for the first and last time, and the three of us moved into a yurt in the woods. At the time, I was only physically disabled in my upper body, my dominant arm in particular, which is an odd thing to navigate in both the disabled and non-disabled worlds—mostly invisible and massively impactful. My love chopped all the wood and carried all the water. I had to stop working, go on and off various medications, apply for disability, and have three surgeries in three years. I had a rib removed and got to keep the bone. I built a fire in the woods to boil my own meat and the formaldehyde off of it. It was pretty magical and gross.

We had no running water and no internet. Iggy loved it. In the winter we'd wake up most mornings to the creaking of the woodstove door with awe and worry for this small child creating fire from last night's embers. They loved peeing outside and exploring the forest. They were never afraid to go to the outhouse at night by themself. We played *Ocarina of Time* from the Zelda series on the couch together, the beginning of our video game bonding.

When we moved to the yurt, I expected that my pain would get better, not worse. I envisioned large gardening and outdoor construction projects. I didn't know yet that I had developed CRPS in my right arm after my first surgery. During our four years at the yurt, we showered at our neighbors' house, in their second-floor bathroom. One day, I bent over slightly to adjust the water temperature, and I felt, and heard, a deep thump in my pelvis. I could barely stand back up or move at all. Somehow, I made it back to our couch and laid flat on my back for several days. This event spread the CRPS to my leg and led me to get my diagnosis, finally. My ability to walk has declined slowly since then.

By saving some money from living in the yurt and applying for a few first-time home-buyer programs, we were able to get a mortgage for a small house off the side of Interstate 95. It's one large room, two small bedrooms, a bathroom, and a backyard with deer. It's my precious pain palace and our whole world these days. I don't live in the fantasy that it is something we earned or necessarily even deserve, other than the fact that all humans deserve stable housing. We are white privilege–receiving settlers on stolen Wabanaki land, and I'm sure that is a major reason we were approved for any kind of loan. I endeavor to balance a hypocritical, enormous daily gratitude for this place with fervent dreams and work toward a decolonized, racially just, and anti-capitalist future.

Disability justice is a powerful movement led by disabled queer and trans, Black, Indigenous, and people of color who created the most intersectional and revolutionary framework I've ever encountered, and it has changed my life radically. I truly owe my life to these luminary artists, writers, and organizers, and I know I'm not alone. Patty Berne, one of the original founders of Sins Invalid and Disability Justice, wrote:

> A Disability Justice framework understands that all bodies are unique and essential, that all bodies have strengths and needs that must be met. We know that we are powerful not despite the complexities of our bodies, but because of them. We understand that all bodies are caught in these bindings of ability, race, gender, sexuality, class, nation state and imperialism, and that we cannot separate them.

This framework does not allow anyone to be disposable. From being raised in an ableist and otherwise oppressive society, even with my intersecting privileges, I have been ready to throw myself away at moments in my life. By connecting to the work of this movement, I have learned that my queer disabled body has a revolutionary value just by existing as it is. My perspective outside of non-disabled life is important. I am part of a vibrant culture and history that disabled people and people with chronic illness have been creating for generations. As I move away from defining myself by what my body and mind can or can't do, I move toward feeling like I am enough as I am. This is the strength I show Iggy now, the strength I never knew I'd have.

* * *

My father is also disabled, born deaf in 1950, the child of Greek immigrants. Because of class, language barriers, and xenophobia, he never had access to the Deaf community, ASL, or other resources and support. I witnessed the audism and dehumanization he experienced often growing up—and still does. He is also the hardest-working and most self-sacrificing person I've ever met. I've learned so much from him.

My mother, an Irish ex-Catholic hippie, was a very involved and hardworking parent too. When I became a parent, I had no roadmap for what it would look like for me, but I called on my parents' wisdom in me for direction. They taught me and my brother loyalty to our commitments, to work all of the time and never be still. As much of a gift as that was, I'm still excavating those values from my disabled heart. Disability justice anchors me in the truth that the worth of my body is not a component of profit, and I must pace myself to be sustained long-term. Those truths teach me not only to accept my frequent and undeniable need for rest but to celebrate it.

I am not the parent who can show up to every event, make dinner, drive, or even sit up with my eyes open sometimes. The armchair I write this from is the gravitational center of our home. We have a banner over the TV that says, "Stay Cozy." We take coziness very seriously in our family. It is how we bond together and show love to ourselves and each other. It is also what I need and often all I have to offer. In an interview Michelle Obama did with Oprah, the former First Lady talked about the importance of letting her children see her weaknesses and imperfections. She explained that if you want your children to share their vulnerability with you, you must show them that it is okay to be vulnerable; telling them is not enough.

Though I see myself as a steady rock in my family, I am sick and in pain around my child every day. I am afraid that if I show any more vulnerability to them, they will feel as if they need to care for me. How do I offer them the courage of vulnerability while assuring them that they are secure in my care? Ultimately, I'm learning, it is not in my control. And that is okay. The best I can do is offer my honesty and resist my instincts to hide. I am the parent who is committed to showing up in my flawed humanity, who will keep checking in with them about what is emotionally true, and who will make sure they have access to therapy when they need it.

Iggy and I still play video games together. They give me game-based assignments to complete while they're at their dad's house. I think it affirms for them that they're still my top priority even when they're not here. When I went through a chronic pain management program at the local hospital, one of the doctors told us about a study that showed playing video games can reduce the volume of pain signals being sent to the brain, and it has the added benefit of initiating Iggy into a nerd culture that will hopefully be a life ring for their gloriously odd self in middle school. They love Dungeons & Dragons and graphic novels and are in a theater company that encourages their confidence and newly identified nonbinary gender. They're way ahead of me already. Last summer they started synchronized swimming, too. Unsurprisingly, they have a natural talent for it. They've been choreographing dances in lakes and rivers since before they could swim. It was, in a way, a compromise for the dance classes they asked for. I thought the water would be gentler on their body than the punishing hardwood floors and mirrors of dance. Dance broke my body and my heart, and I struggled to allow Iggy to enter that world.

One of my primary diagnoses is Ehlers-Danlos Syndrome, the hypermobility type. It is a genetically inherited connective tissue disorder. It's responsible for my unstable joints, widespread pain, GI dysfunction, dizziness, occipital neuralgia, and more. Iggy shows the common early signs of extreme and prolonged "growing pains" and hyperflexibility.

When I was a young dancer, I didn't know why I was nearly always injured or sick. I was not raised to acknowledge or investigate the needs of my body in that way. I was taught to just keep going. I strained my body in every imaginable way. I malnourished myself for almost two decades, valued pain and extremes in movement, and was applauded for it. One of my last staged pieces featured a striptease and slamming my body into a wall several times. That's art, right? I was way too flexible and stretched every joint past its limit. I have to protect Iggy's body from that kind of socially praised self-harm. I have to show them how to love the weight and limitations of their body and, quite possibly, how to live a full young disabled life.

Sometimes I think that means never letting them witness my grief or struggle with severe pain. I don't want to scare them. I don't want them to see me and fear their future. I want to trust that they will experience more self-love than I did. I know for sure that they won't have the same journey as me. It is clear to me that most of my chronic pain was caused by the medical industry not knowing what was going on and cutting into me anyway. If I had those experiences so that they don't have to, it will have been worth it.

In the hours before I'm able to haul myself out of bed, my partner, Eden, walks our dog in the truly lovely industrial wasteland that surrounds our home. Since schools have closed, Iggy has been going with them. I hear about the two of them getting lost and having adventures. Eden told me about a conversation they had on one of their mornings outside. They told Iggy that they'd forgotten how nice it was to have company on their walks.

"I used to go on a lot of walks with your mama," they told them, "and it's nice to be able to go on walks with you now."

"I like going on walks with you too," Iggy responded, the kid who has complained for years about being forced to go on walks at their father's house.

Hearing about this sweet moment between them flooded my chest with opposing waves of feeling, a duality that I am extremely familiar with. The gratitude I have for my family, for the relationship between my partner and my child, is immense. It keeps me alive. The ways that they care for each other and for me are immeasurable and affirm that we have done something right in this life by finding each other. Simultaneously, I could fall through the earth with the grief of knowing that I will never climb a mountain with them, explore the woods, or traverse uneven terrain with them. My father took me up several mountains as a kid. It was part of who he was, and he could share it with me. He showed me how to climb steep rocks safely, to lean into the wind. The loss engraved in the words "I will never" is vast, and there are many things I will never do with Iggy—never do again at all.

Last spring, on one of the first warm days, when the snow had finally melted a bit, we drove out to our favorite state park on the northern shore of Sebago Lake. It was early enough in the season that the road to the campground site was still closed off to cars. Eden set up my collapsible electric wheelchair on the other side of the road block and parked so I could walk around to it with my cane. Iggy brought their new toy bow and arrow set and packed a tube of Pringles into the pouch on the back of my chair. They shot arrows ahead of us and picked them up as we went. The road was so beautiful to pass down slowly. Tiny waterfalls from the snowmelt trickled over boulders on either side. There was a bog filled with red bushes and a sign that marked off a large section of the woods as Gay Meadow. We celebrated this by naming the trees after our favorite queer musicians and drag queens.

When we got to the campground beach, I left my chair on the last hospitable stretch of path and walked with my cane to a large stump. The lake stretched huge and sparkling out in front of us, cradled by gray-blue mountains in the distance. Eden had given Iggy their old digital camera that morning, and they ran around filming clips of their bare feet in the sand. I pocketed three pebbles to remember this precious moment secluded in nature and tried to imagine what kind of equipment we would need to go camping here again in an accessible way for me. Eden thought we'd need a spot close to the bathrooms, but I said I'd rather be closer to the water. Iggy agreed.

Being a mother and becoming disabled are the hardest things I've ever done. I am always navigating how to balance my body's full-time need for self-care and parenting's ongoing demands of self-sacrifice. I roll in and out of radical self-love and acceptance and the struggle of inevitably doing it imperfectly. I want Iggy to know me as flawed, to hear me apologize when I'm wrong and say I don't know. Having a disabled parent has given Iggy a respect for the realities of their own body and the boundaries of others. They are instinctively caregiving and empathetic, things that they will have to learn how to keep balanced in their life as they grow but are already starting to grasp. They are good at quiet and stillness. They are never bored. They defy convention and authority and expect to be treated with dignity and respect. Unapologetically powerful and radical women, queer people, and social and racial justice activists are their icons. They make space for hard feelings and accept that multiple truths can exist about something at once. I wish we had more models for how sick and disabled parents exist day-to-day in our families, but I guess, like queerness, it's a challenge that is beautiful because we are free to create it for ourselves.

At night, we usually eat on the couch and watch cartoons. Sometimes Eden will turn my armchair around so that we can play a game together at the table. Iggy will roll the dice for me on my turn and hand me any cards or the change for my Steven Universe Monopoly money. I still read Iggy to sleep every night. When I get into bed with them, they'll usually pour out the worries of their heart to me. I'm so grateful for their trust. If the worries are particularly big, I'll help them cast a protection spell around the bed, banishing anything they don't need tonight and saving tomorrow's troubles on the other side of their bedroom door. Some nights they grab my head, like an emotional Greek uncle, and say: "I love you more than anyone in the world, I don't know what I would do without you, you are the best mama, and you do so much for me."

I usually respond by telling them that they're the best kid in the world and that I love them at least fifty percent more than they love me. It's funny to watch how strict and earnest they get when I compete with them like this. I'm often a few sentences into the novel we're reading that night when I interrupt myself to say: "Oh, Iggy, *kala nihta*, good night." They'll wake up just enough to race me to say the second half: "*S'agapó polý tolmadáki mou.*" I love you so much, my little stuffed grape leaf.

MAYBE: THE MOTHERHOOD THING
STELLA CARRUTHERS

All kids run and fall. If they're not hurt too badly, they pick themselves up again. Often, they stand still a moment, deciding whether it hurts enough to cry. A quick survey of the area for a sympathetic adult often plays a big part in this decision. Sympathetic adults give out plasters and hugs. They kiss hurt knees better, and we all want to be Better. However, most of the time, kids decide they are okay. They run on. Back to games of Follow the Leader and Tag You're It and Mother's and Father's.

For the record, I was a terrible follower. I never stepped in time. I got distracted by things like butterflies and younger kids swinging super high on the swings. I also always ended up standing on the shoelaces of the friend in front of me. But the real reason I was such a bad follower was that I hated not knowing where I was going. I liked to see What Came Next.

The What Came Nexts could be something like turn left at the jungle gym and head to the tennis courts. Innocent enough. But it could also be to head down through the forest at the bottom of the playground. This forest was Out of Bounds, according to the teachers. And as a Good Kid, I tried to do what the teachers said. But we still went there. Well, the other kids did. And when I was following a leader, I went there too. I followed because that was what you are meant to do. Even though I hated the forest because it was dark and damp and smelled like an armpit.

I like to think that the What Came Nexts can serve as a metaphor for how I've so far approached living. I have always tried to be the leader of my own life. Independent to a fault, some would say. I've turned toward brightly lit, tennis-court kinds of places often enough. And that has been nice. Great even. But even with myself leading my life (or maybe because of it, now I come to think of it), I've also entered dark, fairy tale forest–like places and gotten lost in them for months, even years, at a time. I've felt cold and wet and miserable, and I haven't been able to see how I relate to the world in any kind of normal sense.

The thing I have smelled then has been Fear. Fear of being stuck in the forest. Fear of never getting out and living in the dark forever. I have also been fearful of being found out as a fake. You know, a pretender of a person who is found out for all she isn't. Then there was the fear of feeling things too much ... or too little ... sometimes for even not feeling anything at goddamn-all. I also felt Fear of being the person who breaks the line by falling over and then crying. And following that was Fear of never being able to stop crying...

When I was a kid, I once dashed headlong into a metal pole when playing tag. I was lucky. No broken nose. Just a headache and a heck of a lot of hurt pride. I remember this fall in an intensely physical way. The rough, gritty concrete smearing my small, pale knees bloody. The watery winter light shafted through purple clouds. How my hands stung, rough-red. I also remember how I slowly picked myself up again, brushing the grits of gravel from my skin, rubbing my sore hands on my tacky wool winter skirt. I remember feeling angry at the pole for being there. For existing. For making me feel stupid in front of the school yard. I was also angry at myself. For letting myself be hurt.

But I did not cry. Even though I really, really wanted to. Because this was my first lesson in Hiding Hurts. It is something I'm great at now. I have made it an art form, along with the other women in their early thirties trying to figure their shit out in the name of a quarter-life crisis.

I pretend it doesn't hurt that I'm single once again while my peers are getting married and thinking about starting families. I pretend that on the days I forget to take my meds, it doesn't feel like the world is peeling off at the edges like an old Band-Aid so that even the touch of the air hurts a bit. I pretend that I am totally content with academics and books and black turtleneck tops because that is what literary people are meant to wear to look cool. Or something.

Hiding Hurts is all about Making Pretend. And we get well trained in that as kids. We pretend to be mothers and fathers who raise kids and clean houses and go to office jobs and drive cars and hold babies like the precious, wriggling things they are. As a pretend mother, I remember laying out leaf platters and kowhai seeds as pretend meals because a big part of being a mother is nourishing both body and mind. In my version of pretend motherhood, we were eating plant-based before it was even a thing.

As a pretend mother, I wanted to do it fully, properly. This was the case with everything I did, pretend or otherwise. I wanted to do it well. To the best of my ability. So, I wiped away imaginary poo and safety-pinned handkerchiefs as diapers. I burped plastic dolls as practice for when I would be a mother in real life. I saw these, in my seven-year-old eyes, as important things to know.

Because, in these games, I was always A Mother.

I always assumed the role of looking after my plastic babies and my classmates pretending to be my children. I kissed my seven-year-old husband on the cheek and wished him off to A Good Day's Work and then embraced him with a hug that said Welcome Home. While he was At The Office, I did housework, cleaning away leaf skeletons with a broom made from twigs. I wiped down surfaces. I dusted away cobwebs. I followed the actions I'd seen on TV that meant I kept A Nice Home. Because somehow, even at seven, I modeled the life of a 1950s housewife. Talk about an early indoctrination of gender roles.

And it wasn't from my own mother. She was a bohemian landscape architect who actively enjoyed her work and her role as a mother. To me, my mother modeled the life of having, if not all, then lots of it. An interesting job that worked for a greater good: planetary survival through park plans and tree plantings. The kids, a boy and a girl, both at once when she discovered she was carrying twins. She also had the creative fulfillment of flowers.

* * *

As adults, we also Make Pretend. We utilize the skills we've mastered as kids. As adults we Make Pretend that we are okay. Especially when we aren't. I, for example, pretend that I'm happy alone. That I'm happy in a low-wage job. That I'm happy living the quiet life I've been led to believe is the only one my health allows. But at heart, often secretly, even to my daily-living surface self, I want someone to wake up next to. My last relationship ended on okay terms, but it ended a while ago now, and there has been no one since. I want someone to share tea and toast with. Someone to go out dancing with until the early morning while we sweat our days away. Someone to tell me I'm doing okay. And, because he'll be there, I will be okay.

I also like to think that I could be truthful about my okay-with-this to my hoped-for partner. And because of this, I could stop fucking pretending. Pretending that money is not a worry. I could stop taking pride in frugality when it's just being poor. I could stop pretending that on my bad days my thoughts don't jump around like teeny-bopper concertgoers and the world is a drunk rock star falling over itself in front of Everyone Who Matters.

However, as someone who is often not okay (and rarely truthful about it), I try to tamp down an inherent restlessness that has me dreaming of Other Cities and Other Lives.

It always stays with me, though, this restlessness for Other. Because even when I try to weigh myself down, I still seek out what living differently might mean for me. In retaliation, I read heavy academic feminist books from the library at the university where I work. They literally help weigh me down and tamp the restlessness, at least in a physical sense.

They also tell me that how I'm living is fine, how for many creative bohemians it might be The Goal. Part-time work to support a creative life. Time to write in. The independence of being beholden to no one. Living alone, where I can keep my own hours and not be accountable to anyone else. However, I'm not sure if this lifestyle is The Goal I want to work toward for myself any longer. And that leaves a hell of a lot of questions and very few answers.

The questioning and seeking for answers of this isn't-kind-of-living, for me anyway, comes down to issues of Give and Take. And a big one for me as a woman in her early thirties is how when you live with a disability, the idea of having a family becomes a tug-of-war between wants and hopes, needs and realities. You might want kids. You want to carry a child in the pear of your uterus. To feel kicks from the inside out. To grow and glow like a golden peach.

I, for one, am not so sure. I love kids with their clear-eyed questions and creative verve for living. But babies terrify me. Their fragility and vulnerability. Those translucent skins and huge eyes. The keening call of their cries.

If I decided I wanted to be a mother, I would carry a huge hope for a healthy baby who hadn't inherited my condition. I would hope for an easy pregnancy. You know, not too puke-y in the early months and not too much weight gain. No complications. I would hope I'd stay well while I carried my child to term. That I'd not run mad. That I'd eat enough fiber. Get enough iron. That the medications I'd had to tail off because they would hurt the fetus wouldn't have been the only thing keeping me sane. That the ones they now put me on wouldn't hurt my baby. Because even doctors don't know everything. I would hope to have a natural birth—and that I'd be able to withstand the stretches of pain. I'd hope for a smiling, pastry-like baby, all sugar and gold.

I know that I'd need special clinical monitoring. I'd need extra support. A psychiatrist. A therapist. A loving partner who would let me cry over cleaning product ads and buy me pickles and licorice at midnight from the all-night grocery store so my cravings could be met.

I'd need plenty of time to tail off my meds before I even started trying for a baby. Months. Years, even. I'd need time to see how much the meds soothed my mind. How much of it was chemical intervention and how much of it had been lifestyle change? The yoga. The early nights. The largely plant-based diet. The poetry reading, early, as the light yawns open from the day.

I'd have to face the reality that having a baby for me is not as simple as stopping birth control and having some hot sex. There would be appointments with maternal mental health professionals. Reality would be the weights and measures taken of drugs and their effects on my mind and my body.

Reality would, in stark truth, probably mean me not being so well for a while. Whether the medication withdrawal symptoms (antidepressant withdrawal can make you feel like shit, apparently, and it can go on for a long time) or an episode of mad, I'm not sure what I fear the most. Feeling like shit physically or acting batshit crazy...

And within that crazy, while The Depression is like crawling through kindergarten paste, the gray snotty sort, every single day for months on end, I fear the mania more. Because of The Repercussions. The spending sprees, the forgetting of Societal Rules. The Fear that the world will run away from me, and I'll never be able to catch up.

Reality is wholeheartedly about my Fear. Of getting sick again. Of not being able to be the kind of mother I would want to be. Reality is how, if I get to the point of peeing on sticks, maybe I won't want two lines to appear, because the fear of being a bad mother clutches me close. It is about trying to hide this tight fear from my lover. It is also about trying to hide it from myself.

I deal with these Fears with long walks in the hills, rock stars screaming in my ears. I wear slogans emblazoned across my chest in stretch cotton. Exclamations of girl power. And ones of feminism. Because maybe I don't need to be a mother. I'm more than a baby maker. I've got a career and a good figure and Doc Martens boots. I'm going places.

I might not need it, but right now, apparently on the wrong side of thirty with the biological clock ticking, I wonder if I do want it. Because not being a mother is another thing I will have missed out on because of my health.

And the idea of living with that loss is fucking hard.

I'm a millennial. I was raised to think that I could have it goddamn-all. Kids. A lover. A great job. Six-pack abs. Time for fiber craft hobbies and gym sessions and printmaking workshops.

As a feminist, I don't want to be told I can't. And while I haven't been told this by an individual doctor, the Western medical model implies it in certain ways, and that feels like I'm failing once again at Normal Life.

Even worse are the words "you shouldn't." Because "shouldn't" has a weight of judgment and morality that weighs heavily on the spirit. "Shouldn't" because the world does not need more crazy women or manic men. "Shouldn't" because people with mental illness should never procreate. Nicholson, Sweeney, and Geller wrote about motherhood and mental illness in a 1998 article in *Psychiatry Online* and stated, "The normal desire to bear and raise children is undermined by negative societal attitudes." It is now over twenty years since this piece was written, and those societal attitudes still stand strong. Cultural models regarding illness and disability tell us narratives of ableism where difference is almost always considered to be a bad thing, particularly in relation to parenthood.

Then there is the worst "shouldn't" of all. The "shouldn't" that implies that I cannot handle it. "It" being Motherhood. Admittedly, this particular worry of a "shouldn't'" and a "cannot" is one of a deeply personal nature. Because I wonder how much of it is me and how much of it is social conditioning from the old white men doctors who enforce the allopathic medical model.

Then there is my busyness in life where I just try to get by. I rarely have time to research alternatives in health care and therapeutic intervention. And even if I do, I rarely know where to go to explore these further. This barrier is both an access and an attitude issue.

There is also the idea that has crept up on me about how some of my worries around motherhood might even be masking or acting in a way that I can claim to be a Valid Excuse to say no to kids. Because I have creative dreams and a whole lot of a thing called Ambition.

I then end up questioning my validity as not only a might-be-mother but also a nice, authentic human being (because women are meant to want kids, aren't they?). This doubt even leads me to questioning my identity as a creative person, that thing I have held on to through it all. Because if I use writing as an excuse to not have kids, does that taint it somehow? And does maybe not wanting to have kids make me a bad person anyway? Is a childless woman selfish? Or is she smart when children might take away her very essence, that which makes her not only who she likes to be but also her ability to be a mostly functioning adult human in contemporary society?

I then think a bit more. I consider the late nights and the early mornings. And how babies always seem to cry. I think about how I just do not function without enough sleep. Then there are the constant demands on your time. On your energy. On your stretched-to-skin body. There's also that constant sucking need for love. And not just any kind of love. A Mother's Love. That all-consuming, giving kind of love that ends one kind of living and starts another.

The worst thing is that sometimes I do believe the Shouldn'ts. Because somewhere along the way, I have learned that mental illness is bad. It means weakness. A fault of the spirit. A fault, even, in the self. Because in our world of the West, doctors do know best. They have six-plus-year degrees. They Know Things. Important Things. They know how to measure life's blood. They know how to listen to heartbeats. They are the ones who are given the task and responsibility to diagnose our deaths. Physically, yeah, like cancer. But there's another kind of death. A quieter kind. And I experience this kind of death when I'm out in the city and I see a bouncing baby on a knee or a sleeping kid in a stroller. It's the death of a certain version of myself. A version I'm not sure I want. But it is also one I'm not sure I don't want, either.

* * *

Meanwhile, Betty Boop rests on my boobs while I sleep each night. I don't do lacy negligees. No one to wear them for, anyway, right now. And I'm too self-conscious to sleep naked. Oversized, cartoon-emblazoned T-shirts will do. Betty is hopeful about babies and breasts and boys. But she's a cartoon pinup. She's never had to worry about any of this kind of shit. She's a good bedmate. Quiet. Doesn't move. Or breathe too loudly. She just reaches into my dreams…

Swirls them into hot-pink, glitter-card love-hearts and red roses and white silk camisoles and coconut body lotion and gentle wake-up kisses from sexy long-legged lovers and lone coffee shop poetry dates with myself and expensive but practical shoes and weekend lie-ins that last the whole day and fancy pasta in plastic packets because I can afford handmade gnocchi as an Independent Woman. She dreams for me, in a house that is quiet to return to. It is a place of retreat and rest so I can recharge and better face life when I need to.

In this dream life, I can rise early for work and know my lunch is the only one that needs making. And that if I'm running late, I can afford to buy a salad because I have that thing called Expendable Income. I do laundry once a week. And it's never that dirty. When I want kid time, I can visit with friends or relatives. The great part about this is that at the end of the day, I can hand them back.

Betty has me dreaming of the life I could have Without. And it doesn't seem so bad. I can fill it with all sorts of other things. Those that don't grow out of clothes and cry and shit and piss like kids do. But these things won't love me back. And a child will do that every minute of every day. They will also love you after you're gone.

Lovers love you, too, sure. But not in the same all-or-nothing, literally-will-love-you-forever kind of way that children do. Kids can make you immortal. Children can make you feel like every day is lived forever because of the sheer scale of The Love. The huge, consuming, perfect-pink, perfume-cloud of sweet-scented love. And sometimes I really want to both eat and inhale and be overwhelmed by that love. I really, really do.

But then there is Betty whispering about freedoms and fancies where men listen to me giggle and love my legs, and I love that they listen to and love these things about me. They probably won't love me, though, when I am crying on the bathroom floor, trying to be quiet so no one else knows. I make sure no one knows about how uncertain I am. About this maybe-motherhood thing.

* * *

If my normal emotions are so turbulent that they need to be managed by medical intervention, then I worry about the feelings motherhood might bring forth. The UK mental health advocacy organization Mind supported a guest blogger in 2019 who wrote that "the fundamental emotions of parenthood are so strong that their distortions are powerful and destructive too." I worry about this idea of inviting in more powerful feelings to my life, where emotional management is already necessary. These feelings have the potential to bring great joy and love, and that is wonderful, but I am deeply afraid of the potential for a new level of destructive emotional experience.

* * *

I'm not sure I am prepared to risk exposing a child to that level of emotional instability. I think I only want to be a mother if I can do it The Best Way. And I'm anything but The Best. A blogger for Scary Mommy asks, "What do you do when your best is barely hanging on?" I am fortunate that my best in recent years has been a lot better than that. But I fear that with a baby my level of best would disintegrate, and not only would I be barely hanging on, I'd also lose a sense of what there was to hang on to. As is the nature of my mood disorder, when I am unwell, I lose perspective on life. I get confused about what the good times mean. The great times get warped by mania. I fear the bad times I find myself in. And I remember that there might be worse to come...

The Better Days for me at present mean three meals eaten slowly. Every day. They mean being able to read in bed and not just fall exhausted onto the pale, petaled sheets. They mean wearing clothes that make me feel good. Blue skinny jeans with button-up blouses. Dark pinafore dresses and silk shirts. A mustard yellow knitted beret.

And I wear red lipstick every day, even while vacuuming. Every moment of my day holds the promise of a sticky-colored kiss. It's a way of living reverentially for me. It also differentiates me from the six-month, gray-sweatpant, bare-face, hack-haired Depression of my twentieth year.

I also hold the colored promises of kisses on my lips as an ode to Beauty. The Princess who, in The Stories, was cursed to sleep for one hundred years. I've been asleep, too, in a Jungian psychology archetypal way. And I feel I'm just waking up again now. In my story, I am a Princess waking up to the whole goddamn-beautiful world.

And that world feels wonderful and large and full of possibility.

Yet, at the same time, while my love for the world is expansive, and I am excited for what I can mean to it, I'm also longing for the smaller intimacy of a cute guy who kisses me in greeting, wherein his kiss acts as both an acknowledgment (you're here, you're pretty, I like you) and as a promise (I will return to you with take-out curry and your body on my mind.)

But I have a Big Fear here, too. That I, alone, will not be enough for him. He'll say it's okay. He chooses me. Me with the breasts and the hips and the lipstick lips and great vegan cooking skills. He chooses me with the suitcase full of notebooks and the one-room studio bedsit that has a million-dollar view. Not that he looks at that when he is over. He only has eyes for me.

But I worry.

I worry that as I get older and my friends start birthing babies, he'll get itchy-footed and twitchy-hearted. Will want to be a Baby Daddy rather than just the cool uncle or some kid's parents' friends. And I worry I'll feel the same way. That I'm missing out on things. That I've failed somehow. As a lover. As a nonexistent mother. As a woman.

But the thing I'm most frightened of is a different kind of worry. You see, I really, really fear I won't be enough for myself. And that, I think, is the worst kind of loneliness. Because if a lover leaves, it sure as hell hurts, but there's chocolate and Julia Roberts movies from the 1990s and break-up songs and fluffy animal-feet slippers and friends who bring mega bags of potato chips and tissues that look like blossoms and that smell like my grandmother did.

But when you are not enough for yourself, you're left in a dark little corner of identity. And it hurts to be there because when the light comes, you are not used to it, and it blinds you.

So, I rarely risk anything relating to dating or men. An exciting Friday night for me is takeaway pizza from a place called Hell and seeing who will die or have gratuitous sex on *Game of Thrones* this week. I own beautiful shoes and pretty dresses. One of my tops is even velvet. It is pink. It looks like a rose petal. But I've never worn it. Because it's a Date top. And I almost never go out on dates.

I haven't let myself be relationship-status positive again because of the level of truth I have to articulate about having kids and being chronically ill and taking medication and how hard this can feel a lot of the time. So instead, I sit by myself in my little one-room studio bedsit and listen to punk rock songs as I write. The words and the heavy beats help with the hurt a bit. But it's a small bit.

* * *

I started out writing this essay about kids looking around the playground when hurt for a sympathetic adult to cry to. To be comforted by. To be kissed better by.

I define "sympathetic adult" here as someone supporting a certain level of kindness. The dictionary definition of "sympathy" also uses the words "consoling," "condoling," and "commiserating." These are definitive words I like less.

Now as an adult myself, I want to be perceived as sympathetic. I want the cultivated kindness (toward self and others) that wanting to want kids gives me. No matter that it is shaped from a level of societal expectation that doesn't take into account circumstance.

Because of this expectation and its associated cultural framework, I want to want that deep-devoted, unflinching-forever kind of love mentioned earlier. The love you feel for your children. And that they feel for you.

I don't, however, want to be on the other side of sympathy. The kind of sympathy that condoles and commiserates. I do wonder, however, whether I may have to settle for sympathy in terms of its consolatory elements.

I worry that if it gets out that I might not be able to have kids because of mental illness I'll get The Look. Not the one of wide-eyed approval. I can deal with the fucked-up-ness of that perception of responsible action. Think, mental illness equals hereditary condition equals must not procreate. It's a fucked equation, but at least there is some kind of crazy (I use this word here on purpose) logic to it. Even if it's one built on the fear-and-scare of mental illness being an inherently bad thing. In my experience, mental illness is a pretty damn sucky thing. But despite societal judgments, I am gradually learning to accept that it has also made me who I am today. And I genuinely like that woman.

The sympathy I fear is the kind that builds on my weaknesses. My fear that I'd be a bad mom. That I'd get sick again and not be able to look after my kids. My fear that my level of "normal" functioning is so below other people's that I'd not be able to keep up with children and all that raising kids entails. The late-night feedings as young babes. The early mornings when they're still young and they jump on me because they want cartoons NOW! And then later, the ferrying to extracurricular activities. Sports. Art. Music. Even later is the worry over teens out late doing God-knows-what.

I fear that the emotional pull of that huge kind of kid-love will be too much for me and my mood-disordered mind and I'll collapse into a soggy heap. I know what it is to be emotionally wrung out. And it is a place I promised myself I would never go back to. This is a promise I cannot necessarily keep to myself, but I still made it. And I still hold myself to it. It was, on reflection, more a vow than a promise. And although I am nonreligious, I stick to my vows. I also try to keep my promises. So, I hold myself twice accountable here.

A vow is defined as a dedicated promise. And if I am anything, I am dedicated. My school reports consistently stated my dedication to my studies. I called myself diligent in my approach to undergrad. I never pulled an all-nighter. I got every assignment in by the due date.

The lowest grade I got was a B+. It was for sociology. I loathed learning about the Protestant work ethic even though I exhibited it in my application to my studies. I thought Marx seemed like he'd be a cool dude. Rebellious. Outspoken. Probably kind of hot in a rebel-rebel black-haired-hero kind of way. I liked his spirit of challenge. His democratic approach to work and rights.

If Marx was my man, I'd probably just say fuck it. Fuck them. Fuck them and their slam-the-door-shut views. Their small-mindedness. How they can only see within the limits of boxed-to-dark rooms. These rooms are kept shadowed by hulking prejudice and a huge amount of lack of understanding that blocks out any kind of natural light. But when I do hold my life up to daylight, the words that tell my story blur because they are backlit, and my eyes have not had time to adjust. I am sometimes not sure what they say exactly anymore. And worse, on my bad days, I'm not sure I want to know.

* * *

Sometimes parenting with a disability means that you don't. And that is a loss, because I can make fairy costumes out of curtains. I know how to make angel-wing cupcakes. I can dig a great moat. I love car chases, especially when I decide to make car noises. I think mud is made to jump in. I covet kid's clothes in all their bright shouts of color. I adore reading stories aloud. And I apparently give out quite good hugs.

My What Came Next is uncertain right now. And I am finding that harder than I like to admit. I've been thinking of going to graduate school to study writing. Until recently, I'd been set to follow this path in a southern city. But now with COVID raging rampant and violent protests about mandates in my home country of Aotearoa as well as the Ukraine conflict and the ongoing climate crisis, I feel like I might want the stability of a known city in an increasingly uncertain world.

To live in a caring manner toward myself is, I feel, essential if I am to have any hope of caring for kids in the future. And writing is how I process, interact with, and make sense of the world. If I do decide I want to be a mother, writing will be an essential part of keeping myself well. It is not only an identity moniker. It is also therapeutic in that it helps me be the person I want to be. She is more compassionate and kinder and less worried about everything. All these qualities are ones I would hope to cultivate as a mother.

So, in a gesture toward being the best version of myself, both now and moving into the future, I am looking into online writing classes I can take from home. I am also investigating courses at my local universities. At the same time, I continue to weigh up the different pros and cons around leaving or staying. Whether I am childless or a mother, and whether I remain living in the place I know or move away to study, I not only want but need to be a woman who writes. That I am once again divided over an essential question of self, that is, the very place I set my story, feels surprisingly okay. I feel like the Maybe Motherhood thing has helped me develop skills for balancing two different ideas of myself and the kind of life I see myself leading.

* * *

The Maybe Motherhood thing holds a personal loss. And I own that today. It's also a loss of a possible future. Because in my world, you can lose possibilities like loose change you forget about. There is always the chance of finding it again, although you never know when that moment will come. Or if it will come at the right time … if it will come at all. A parental future for me is not a definite "no." But it is also less than a possible "yes" at the same time. It exists in the twilight zone of fears, scares, loves, dreams, and fluttering hopes.

Because I do still have hope. Hope for a certain way of existing in the world where I love myself more often than I don't and can be accepting of the choices I make. Whether that is to follow the gendered norms of motherhood or not, I hope I can be a leader in my life and not follow others because being different feels too hard.

I do, however, also carry a grief. And griefs have the potential to break hearts. I fear the grief will trump the hope I carry and loss will color my world. It will be a loss for the kids I might never have. It will be a loss of a certain sense of myself. And, leading on from that, it will also be a loss to the world for what I might have been. A Good Mother.

DON'T FALL, MISTER

REINE DUGAS

Do you remember the game Don't Break the Ice? There was a red plastic man in the center of a floor of white plastic ice cubes, and the box cover said, "The game begins, the ice is thin. Be careful or you may go in." The goal of the game was to keep the red man from falling through while chipping ice cubes out from underneath him. Whoever let him fall lost. But as long as there were a few pieces, strategically tight and balanced just right, the man could hold.

The pieces of white plastic ice fit so tightly together. You'd be surprised how many could be chipped away before the entire floor collapsed—almost all of them. But still, you just knew that as each one came out, the foundation grew weaker and weaker, and the odds that the man would fall increased every moment. This game always made me anxious. When all the pieces broke and clacked into a pile, the sound made me jump. Also, I didn't want the man to fall in. So, I'd tap gently on the ice cube farthest away from him. Tap, tap, tap. "Don't fall, mister," I'd think when it was my turn.

I think about that game often. I played it in the 1970s, so it's odd that it would ever cross my mind. But the images of the pieces, there one minute, and a gaping hole the next, have stayed with me. And the tapping. Tap, tap, tap. I always wanted the ice to hold.

* * *

In the summer of 2015, I felt a little like an explorer myself when I started researching Alzheimer's disease. This was foreign terrain, and I only knew what I'd read as I scrolled through my morning news feed, or what I'd heard from people who knew someone with Alzheimer's. When I was young, I'd witnessed it with my grandmother, but only long-distance, from 3,000 miles away. When my dad was officially diagnosed—when it became more than a hunch—I needed to really understand.

Alzheimer's is such an abstract disease. Initially, memory loss was all I really knew. Severe and debilitating memory loss, eventually rendering a person unable to care for themselves. Soon, through both research and watching my father's decline, I would come to learn a lot. Things I wished I didn't know.

Most importantly, I'd learn that Alzheimer's is the loss of actual brain matter and function that goes far beyond being unable to remember names or places or past events. *Loss of brain matter and function*—this was hard for me to process, to visualize. I began to realize how powerful memory actually is, because who ever really takes the time to consider the brain? We just accept that it gets us through our days and lives. But the brain and our memory inform and connect *everything* we say, do, and think. The brain is responsible for linking words to ideas, interpreting pleasure or pain, recalling simple and complex information, even, and tragically, controlling something as essential as swallowing.

In my initial research, I came upon an image of a basic pie chart depicting how Alzheimer's impacts the brain. Imagine a full circle with pieces of pie delineated: short-term memory, long-term memory, language, depth perception, motor skills, and so on. In Alzheimer's patients, each piece of the pie slowly deteriorates as time goes by. Short-term memory goes first. Language often goes next. When a person can't recall a word, even though they've said it a million times, it is because the language center is deteriorating. As time progresses, more pieces of the pie disappear.

This simplistic pie chart image helped me understand what was happening to my dad. The progression of his disease was indeed just as the chart claimed it would be. First, his short-term memory started to go. I noticed him telling the same story three or four times over the course of our lunch. He didn't even realize it and would tell each rendition with the same level of enthusiasm, not noticing the confusion on my face—confusion I quickly learned to mask for his benefit. Interestingly, he would remember stories from when he was younger, like that time he hitchhiked from California to New Orleans, and his mother busted him for it. Those would be his long-term memories, still intact a little while longer.

Sometime later, he couldn't understand how to sit in a car. He couldn't bend his body, duck his head, scoot back on the seat, and swing his legs over. Occasionally, he would fall trying to get in, even with us helping. You wouldn't think there were that many movements for a body to make to get into a car. But there are, and they're all stored in the brain. This meant Dad's motor-skill memory was going away. Tap, tap, tap.

One afternoon last July, I remember sitting down with a fresh notebook to read more about Alzheimer's. Both the heat and the humidity were so high, you'd break a sweat if you moved too much. The air conditioner made grinding noises outside my office window as it strained with the effort of keeping my small house cool. There I sat and read up on the disease, made notes on a pad of paper as if I were doing a research project. And maybe I was—the only research project that has ever mattered. Not only did I want to understand Alzheimer's, but I also desperately needed to see if it could be slowed down. I knew I couldn't stop it, but if I could figure out something, anything, that could help my dad ...

I assiduously compared his behavior to my notes to see how he was doing, hoping his disease was not progressing faster for him than the charts said it might. But what kept tripping me up was *how* exactly the disease impacted a person. How could a person's brain essentially disappear? I couldn't fathom how it could affect some parts of the brain and not others. A pie chart wasn't enough; this required a deeper dive.

* * *

If you hadn't already guessed, articles on neurology, disease, and the brain are extremely difficult, especially for someone without a science background. There was no skating through this material. As I read through websites, blogs, academic articles, and scientific research, I focused as though my life depended on it. Or my dad's life. I learned that there are genetic indicators that increase the risk that a person will get Alzheimer's. There are also environmental factors that contribute, like having diabetes. But what exactly happened in the brain?

As a result of either genetics or environment, there were these insidious plaque-like things called beta-amyloid proteins and tau that work together to gather between neurons, eventually interrupting cell function. I imagined Pac-Man gobbling up dots, but maybe it was more like a blob that grew, smothering essential parts of the brain. In either case, the brain takes a hit, piece by piece. The first parts of the brain that are gobbled up are the hippocampus and hypothalamus. The hippocampus is where new memories are made. And because that's also the part that controls how a person moves through space, damage to this section causes disorientation. The hypothalamus is the hormone production spot, which is responsible for letting us know when we're hungry, sleepy, or thirsty.

Next, the amygdala is an interesting little part of the brain. Shaped like an almond, it controls our perception of emotions. This part lets us know if we're feeling sadness, happiness, anger, or love. It's so tiny that you'd think Pac-Man wouldn't notice it, but no. When people with Alzheimer's begin to change personalities or become aggressive, it's usually because this part of their brain has deteriorated.

The cerebellum determines movement and coordination. Once this is affected, a person has a hard time walking, their speech becomes garbled, and they have difficulty sitting up. Are you imagining pieces of ice falling away?

Another area under assault is the frontal lobe, the decision-making and planning center, which helps control impulses and emotions. Then, there's the parietal lobe, at the top of the head, the spot where pain is interpreted and sensory information is processed. You'll sometimes notice Alzheimer's patients who are hypersensitive to touch or pain. For instance, my dad screams if you rub his arm with more than a feather's touch and acts like the shower is hundreds of needles coming at him rather than simply water. That would be his parietal lobe being chipped away. Tap, tap.

There's also the thalamus, which is responsible for sleep regulation. In the beginning, Alzheimer's patients may be confused about when it's time to be awake or asleep. In the later stages, they will sleep all the time. Dad is only awake a few hours a day now.

* * *

It was hard to believe that the brain, this mysteriously complex organ, could be attacked in such a methodical, persistent way. Couldn't it defend itself? And yet, I'd known people who'd gone through cancer, so I should have been prepared for the body's inability to fight disease. Any part of the body can decay, deteriorate, or be destroyed. Of course it can.

I studied this information and understood it. I did. Looking at my notebook, though, and seeing my dad—sitting next to him and watching him—were two different things entirely. I could not reconcile them. Perhaps I was in denial, even after all my research. My logical brain would not override my emotional brain where he was concerned. For instance, I had learned and accepted that the temporal lobe helps a person recognize everyday objects and hold on to new information. In his later stages, Dad forgot how to use a fork and began picking up food with his fingers. I couldn't help thinking, "You know how to use a fork, you've done it for eighty years. Come on. Please. Pick up the fork." I wanted to cry, to hug him, maybe even shout at him. Why couldn't he just do it? He'd taught me how to use a fork, for God's sake…

Of course, I knew why. I'd learned what the research said, what part of his brain had been affected and why. However, I never ran across anything that explained what part of the brain is responsible for denial—when you cannot or will not believe what is in front of you. Why is the brain so goddamn complex?

I hated my own, and I hated my dad's too. Because sitting there, feeding him lunch one day, I could not or would not understand why using a fork was so difficult. It was just a fork, and he'd been using one his whole life.

* * *

Like holding a fork, Dad showed me how to do many things in the course of my life. One of the things he taught me, and that I use to this day, is to make a to-do list.

I was about twenty years old and had just started working for him. Dad owned a small business—a bar supply company. They sold everything but the liquor, he'd say. I became well-acquainted with mixers—Bloody Mary, margarita, sweet and sour—Styrofoam cups, olives, and sip stirs. You name it, we carried it. The company was called Pio Bar Supply, named after my brother. Neither my father nor my brother drank, so I'm not sure how Dad landed on opening a company that serviced bars, but he did.

We sat in his office on my first day, and he gave me the rundown. His desk, by the way, was not visible under all of the crap piled on it. He was a slob—I'll just say it now. Samples of three-compartment trays were stacked behind him, invoices scattered all over his desk. Blue vinyl bank bags unceremoniously tossed on the floor. He cleared a spot on his desk and took out two fresh yellow legal pads. He gave me one.

"Here you go. This is the most important tool you'll ever need in sales," he told me.

"A tablet?" I asked.

"Yes." He nodded. "That and your personality." He winked at me.

"Every morning," he told me, "you make your list of things to do. It doesn't matter how hectic your day is or how little time you think you don't have. Do it. Trust me."

He explained planning and paraphrased Zig Ziglar, "Plan your work and work your plan." Wearing a black Pio Bar Supply shirt, jeans, and a cowboy belt, he talked to me, and I could tell he was excited to have me working with him. We were always close.

I remember him writing MONDAY in all caps at the top of his tablet, and then he made a list of about twenty items. His pencil made soft sounds as it moved over the paper. I always liked his handwriting—box letters, big and bold, just like him. I wrote a few things to do on mine but nothing like his list. He sharpened his pencil, licked the tip.

"Let's meet for coffee this afternoon and see how we did. 5:00 sharp." Dad was sharp in all ways.

This sounded like a challenge to me, and maybe it was, but I finished every damn thing on my to-do list. When we sat down for coffee and both put our tablets down as if we were showing a hand of cards, we both had every item crossed through. Dad smiled at me. I'd done well, not just on my first day, but at working my plan. Removing items off of a list, scratching them through—this represented accomplishment. Completion.

"Now you can start with a blank slate tomorrow morning," he said.

* * *

A blank slate is usually good. Tabula rasa. Starting fresh. Except when it comes to memory. Then it can go either way. Drawing a blank when you've had a long day is one thing. Having nothing where there once was something in your brain is entirely and devastatingly another. What makes it worse is that when parts of your brain are physically chipped away, you can't get them back. And, to date, there aren't a lot of options for counteracting such terrible loss.

If you've lost a physical part of your body or some mechanical ability, huge strides have been made to compensate. For instance, if you are missing a limb, there are excellent prosthetic devices now. Hearing loss? State-of-the-art hearing aids or cochlear implants are now available. For those people who can no longer use their voices, there is text-to-talk technology.

But if you've lost part of your brain, you are likely fucked. Brains cannot be reconstructed. Our understanding of reviving damaged or deteriorated parts is not very deep. And because the brain tells the body what to do, the real, especially cruel, irony is that if you lose part of your brain, you also lose part of your body—or the control of it. In one fell swoop, you've lost mental and physical capability—the two are inextricably tied for those with Alzheimer's.

So, it can't be fixed or stopped.

Because Alzheimer's is not a sexy disease, it doesn't receive the attention it should or the research dollars it needs. Even though around 5.7 million people were living with it in 2018, at present, there are no cures, no repairs, and no real way to diminish its effects. If you have it, you can take only a few medicines that have been available for years—Dad takes Namenda and Aricept—to hopefully slow the progression of the disease.

Frustration abounds. The person who has it feels angry at first, confused later, and blank toward the end. The caregiver is drained, exhausted. Family and friends are upset and want to help, but how? Doctor's visits seem futile. A few questions are asked—what day it is, who the president is—reflexes and blood pressure checked. No breakthroughs ever announced. You leave as empty as when you came. The painfully drawn-out nature of the disease—to experience or watch—is perhaps the most frustrating. A slow-motion fading away of something I've never wanted to fill in, add on, bring back, or revive so much in my life.

Mom, Dad, and I walk back to the car after each doctor's visit feeling defeated. I hold onto his arm as he takes tentative steps. *Don't fall, mister*, I think.

* * *

The Alzheimer's brain does a disappearing act—one that can be researched and understood, but unless we experience it firsthand, it may never really be clear. In the beginning, I could see that Dad was upset. He could tell he was losing his memory, and it angered him. Now, of course, he doesn't know, and it's only hard for us—the ones who love him and see him every day. As we see each new piece of him disappear, it's heartbreaking. Oh, we steel ourselves to be strong around him, but when I left him the other day, I sat in my car and cried for an hour, because I understood that he had stopped walking and probably never will again. Those days are hard. Others are better.

Mom and I talk about it sometimes, about how we are grateful for the parts of Dad we have. Yes, we miss him on an epic level. We miss the husband and father he used to be. *My friend*—I miss my friend too. There's no getting around that Alzheimer's is a crappy hand to be dealt. That it only gets worse. You never get better. *Ever.* As your brain deteriorates, your body shuts down, until you are done.

When I tell people about Dad, they get this sad look on their face and say, "Oh God, I'm so sorry. It sounds terrible."

Something to that effect. I always say, "Yeah, but..." and mention whatever thing I'm grateful for at the moment.

In the beginning, it was, "Yeah, but at least he still knows my name and can talk to me about simple things."

Later, it was, "Yeah, but he still enjoys his favorite meal."

And later, "Yeah, he doesn't know who I am anymore, but he still smiles when I walk into the room."

Every "Yeah, but..." is a piece of ice still there.

I can't tell you how happy it makes me when I tuck him in for a nap and he winks at me and says, "Thank you, sweetheart." Because he still sees me, even if he doesn't know that I'm his daughter or my name is Reine. He senses that I'm a person who loves him. I'll take that ice cube all day long because it means he's here now and he's holding. A lot has been chipped away from Dad's brain now that he's in stage 7, but there is *just enough* to keep him from falling, at least a little longer.

HEARING MY SON'S WORLD
DYLAN WARD

If I could keep my son perpetually as a six-year-old or a five-year-old, or even a four-year-old again, I would. But unfortunately, I can't. This is a harsh truth I've learned in the few years as a parent and stay-at-home father. It brings a jarring clarity to the meaning behind that oft-familiar phrase: "They grow up so fast."

My babbling two-year old son somehow morphed into a happy, articulate six-year-old kid who, thankfully, still finds the world so compelling at every turn. Unlike me, he's not worried about time, nor is he worried about the million little things that I fret over while his young mind and body itch to be on the move. Children are marvelous creatures, and parenthood proffers the joy of seeing these little humans grow and explore and learn, mesmerized by everything around them. As time passes, I find myself increasingly wanting to hold on to these younger years with my son more than ever.

One thing that happened when I became a parent was that people regarded me differently. They smiled at me warmly when they saw me with my son. They gave knowing looks and winks with the unspoken, shared knowledge of the responsibilities and conditions that come with a child: loving them and keeping them safe from harm. As a disabled parent, however, there have been unpredicted hurdles that have made parenting a little more demanding, that have brought my disability to the forefront in ways I hadn't anticipated. They've made me cautious and more guarded. While I love being a parent, I worry how my disability alters my ability to parent.

I don't often think of myself as disabled first. It's really second nature to me, part of my identity that recedes to the background as another piece that makes me whole. I've been fortunate to hear the world distinctively with a hearing aid in my left ear since a young age. My right ear is rendered deaf. I'm also good at reading lips. But as a parent, unexpected situations have heightened my limitations as a disabled person. Essential baby monitors made specifically for hard-of-hearing and deaf parents were impossible to find. So, I'd wake up during the night, reaching out to touch the monitor with my fingers and feel if my son was awake or crying. Nighttime driving became stressful, because I couldn't understand what my son was saying from the dark backseat, his face unclear in the rearview mirror, his lips unreadable. I realized I'll never be able to hear if my son is hurt and crying for help unless I witness it every time it happens. Riding our bikes to school in the mornings, my son pedals fast ahead of me, and when he says something to me, it is of course lost to the wind. There was the heart-stopping moment on the crosswalk when my son darted around me, unsafely. I recognized my error immediately, my failure to shield him from harm and danger. Had he said something to me that I didn't hear?

I don't recall allowing my disability to impact me negatively in my youth, not in the same way it has as an adult. I think I've done well so far, achieving significant childhood milestones, graduating from college, getting married, building a comfortable life with my supportive and loving husband. We have our home and our pets, and we're blessed with our adopted child, whom we love more than anything. But the limitations as a disabled person are more evident now as a parent, and they weigh heavily on me as my son and I age.

There are unforgettable moments that linger deep in my memory. The nerve-wracking day my son arrived into our lives unexpectedly, when we were uncertain if he was here to stay. His giggles of glee at a caterpillar crawling through the grass, him gifting his pint-sized hand for the caterpillar to explore his fingers, tickling him. The newness and nervousness of those first days of preschool and kindergarten and first grade. The excitement at finally figuring out how to pedal his bike without training wheels. Rocking and cradling him as he was miserable and exhausted from his earache, a balled-up tissue in his palm, the heat of his sickly body pressed into my arms. The time he heard his heartbeat, reveling in that discovery, his tiny, humbled voice repeating, "My heartbeat, my heartbeat." The first soccer trophy he won, carrying that shiny thing cradled next to him like a newborn puppy. When he eyed the ocean, his serious expression mixed with trepidation and joy, his little feet running to and away from those wild, frothy waves.

These memories form each day. They are what color my parenthood, where I have special access to an alternate perspective, into a mystical universe that exists only through my son. I can peer through this universe and view the consequential moments that shape him and enrich his life. I never get enough of the delight that sparks in his eyes whenever he sees or learns something new, small reminders of how sensational this earth can be, of how easily we lose sight of it with age. This is what makes being a parent so worthwhile and what deepens my life.

Why, then, does time seem to go by so quickly when you have a child? Do children really age faster? Or is there something else going on? Like a kind of cruel magic that affects only parents, altering time and speeding it in a way that isn't noticeable, until one day, your little toddler is beginning elementary school, and you're wondering what happened to the past five years. At the point your child begins elementary school, the ticking of time shifts and accelerates, propelling faster, and your once-small child turns into an angst-filled, gawky, and rebellious teenager who faces a horizon of unfamiliar discoveries, hurtling toward young adulthood. Here then, they're off on their own somewhere else, immersed among the landscape of a crowded college perhaps, or working in a low-wage, entry-level job, filled with higher aspirations, or if lucky and adventurous, they're spiritedly trekking across the globe through obscure countries. Now your child is out there in the real world, and you're left behind, their hand slipping away.

Stop. Slow down. Please.

Time is a concept I grapple with, of which there never seems to be enough in a day. I always say, "I don't have time," or "there's not enough time." This reluctant struggle with time is something I've dealt with for the better part of the last twenty years or more. As much as I know that time is a construct that shouldn't affect me or make me feel that I can't get everything done, I'm always overwhelmed by it.

But isn't everyone?

Time, or the lack of it, causes me anxiety. There's a sense that I'm not in control of it, and that no matter what or how much I try, I won't achieve important tasks or fulfill elusive goals. How then can I expect as a parent to instill the necessary confidence in my son to succeed when I struggle with my own confidence?

Is it my hard-of-hearing disability that makes me feel this way? Or is it misfortune that I'm burdened with continual apprehension? I don't really know. I've gotten better, I think, in this brief time as a parent, gradually allowing myself to let go of worries. The house isn't spotless. Dishes pile up in the sink. Clothes go unwashed. Short stories remain half-written. A novel sits unfinished. None of that matters. What matters is time spent with my son. I focus wholly on him, on his experiences, what he sees and hears, what needs I must provide for him, of his own worries and fears and triumphs. All this while doing what I can to raise him under careful, loving guidance amid this dark and wild world.

Parenthood is a time to love, to relinquish insecurities. It is the chance to impart mandatory life lessons and grant your child opportunities, perhaps even ones you never had. I imagine this could be intimidating for anyone. I think deep down there's a secret desire in us to be perfect, to be a parent without flaws, to supply our child with as ideal a life as possible. Eventually we learn it doesn't turn out exactly like we want. Perfection isn't attainable. There are obstacles and mistakes to be made. You and your child will both fail and succeed. Your child should see and understand your imperfections. This is how they learn. And this is okay.

I'm naturally an introvert and, as a hard-of-hearing person, I'm perhaps more introverted than the average introvert. I'm painfully shy in groups, both small and large, ones filled with strangers or friends, with multiple voices jumbled in indecipherable conversations. When I'm confronted with these situations, I strategically place myself where I can avoid as many people as possible or attempt to circumvent the pressure and awkwardness of trying to hear someone over the uncontrollable din of voices and noise. Being hard-of-hearing isn't a readily noticeable disability. The oversized tan hearing aid I wore for years as a child has since been replaced by newer technology that's hardly perceptible. Sometimes it gives me a false sense of confidence and I neglect to politely tell others I am hard-of-hearing. There's no apparent mechanical device or cochlear implant, so it's easy for others to mistake me for normal-hearing. I'm a terrible advocate for myself. And often I'll see the moment a person's face changes when I've missed something said, or my response is a bit slower than normal, or I don't respond at all because I never heard anything in the first place. Some people are kind, others convey impatience.

I'm jealous of the ease with which adults and parents talk to one another in public, at the playground, at the trampoline park, museums, any of the noisy places we parents gravitate to with our children. Many times, I've wished I could engage in simple conversation with another parent, to share my son's achievements, to share my frustrations. Yes, I have been able to do this, but it's rare and usually only with close friends. I'm far too insecure to begin a conversation, and after a while, the strain of hearing becomes exhausting. I'm equally jealous of intimate conversations, how people can whisper or speak in barely audible voices. This especially when my son whispers into my husband's ear, the two of them sharing a secret between parent and child. They eventually do share that secret with me, but the point is, I'll never have the luxury of whispers to bond with my son.

As much as I avoid people, I don't think I was always this painfully shy. Or perhaps I was, and I just misremember it. When I was a child, I might have been less afraid, more willing to be part of the group, to make new friends. Somewhere along the way, that confidence began to fade. While I don't regret being mainstreamed, I was a loner in high school and college, mired in the unpleasantries of adolescence, acutely aware of my differences. I retreated to solitude, even from other hard-of-hearing and deaf students. I don't know why I never made any meaningful connections with them. Could I have been more confident? Yes, I would have been, had I allowed myself to be. A small part of me wonders, though, whether I craved the solitude because it seemed necessary and important to me at the time. Whether it fit with my disability and my introverted personality, along with the desire to be a writer. Aren't all writers like this? Living inside themselves with a proclivity for peaceful seclusion to reflect on the idiosyncrasies of life, to ponder its deep meanings?

My son is far from being the introvert that I am. Instead, he is compelled outward by his extroverted personality. He seeks out friends, new and old, in hopes to mingle and socialize whenever possible. It seems he has an insatiable need to never be alone, to never lack engagement with another soul. Where I gladly pull inward to my own quietness, my son eagerly calls out to others, inviting them into his circle of play and friendship. Of course, when he does this, a tiny fear swells up within me, an incessant worry that I'll have to make small talk with another parent whom I may or may not know. There have been days when I was so worried about talking to anyone that I made up excuses for why he couldn't go across the street to play or why he couldn't stop to visit with the other child we encountered on our walk.

This fear was alarming and filled me with guilt. I knew each time I did this, I was doing a disservice to my son, holding him back because of my insecurities. Now, I let him safely cross the street to join his friends or go to the other side of the playground to play, while I divert my eyes and keep my head down, purposefully examining my cell phone, or reading a magazine or a book. See how well I've progressed? Yet, as I've gotten to know parents, I admittedly am a little more willing to embrace the inevitable conversations, somewhat. It's just not something I'm aching to do.

What amazes me about children, especially my son, is how they assemble together as complete strangers on a playground and welcome and accept one another. They'll become instant friends after a few moments as if they've known each other since birth. It's fascinating how children listen to and communicate with each other in this space of play with their childlike mannerisms. Watching my son and other children do this makes me want to be less guarded than I am, less fearful of communicating and listening. But often, as it happens, I shy away from trying to hear.

Hearing and listening are crucial to creating and nurturing relationships. I ponder this often in the relationship I have with my son. Does my disability affect him and our relationship in a way I don't notice? Will it affect him in the future in an unforeseen way? Could I be a better parent if I heard him with unblemished hearing? My son gives me confidence with his extroverted nature, encouraging me to come out of my shell, to be less afraid. In turn, I wish I could be the parent who's instinctively a leader, the one who is a role model for their child, getting out there and taking charge and doing the hard work.

In my quieter way, I try to be a role model for my son. I write about my experiences as a father to him. One day he may read them. I try to set positive examples, showing him and talking about giving back to the community, helping those less fortunate, reminding him how we should not forget them. I volunteer at my son's school, a small measure of my willingness to be involved in his life, a parental presence for him and his friends. When my son sees me at school, he's happy, and this makes me happy.

Becoming a parent has changed how I interact with and experience much of the world. This happens through my son now, in that universe he inhabits, in the way that he sees and hears. There is so much that he is hearing, and he helps me to understand his world through his hearing. Though I can't hear in the same way he hears music, for example, I still get to enjoy it with him, enjoying it as he enjoys it. It's his facial expressions and his body movements as he dances that enables me to experience what he is hearing. But many times, he wants me to hear something and says, "Listen to this, Daddy," and plays a piece of music or a recording that is relevant to him, or he reads something to me in the car that I miss about half of, and I see disappointment leak into his eyes. I remind him again that Daddy can't hear well.

I'm surprised sometimes by what my son does hear, almost as if he has super hearing. The uncanny way he stops in the middle of whatever he's doing and tilts his head to listen. He'll pick up the sound of kids playing outside somewhere or the beloved ice cream truck cruising down the street. How does he hear that? And the more I watch him hear the world around him, the more I realize how much I don't hear it. I wonder about everything I must've missed growing up. Thinking back on it now as an adult, I realize how much the world isn't built for someone who can't hear.

I remember vividly dreading those games as a child, ones where you get to know each other, like the Telephone Game, or the game where everyone shares something about themselves to the whole group. Each person after must remember what everyone before them shared. This was never fun for me. It was worse if I was closer to the end of the circle than the beginning.

Or other times, when closing my eyes for a listening exercise or meditation or reflection, I spent more time thinking and worrying rather than hearing anything usable. Or all the sermons I didn't hear my father preach from the pulpit or the prayers I didn't hear in church while everyone bowed their heads. Working was difficult among hushed voices inside carpeted buildings, the office phone that taunted me like a loathsome relic. Email was a godsend. Why didn't everyone use it?

Outside of work were parties and evenings out with friends at deafening restaurants. The struggle to join the indistinguishable conversations made me resent it all. There was the embarrassing and discomforting yoga session with a friend, contorting my body in strange ways, tension building in my neck each time I moved my head to read the yoga instructor's lips. It never fails at the dentist office that I can't understand what they're saying with their mask-covered mouth. The bewildering plexiglass that infuriatingly softens the bank teller's voice; the garbled speaker at the drive-thru; the non-captioned videos on the computer. When I'm out somewhere, sometimes I turn and realize a stranger has been talking to me or has asked a question, and they're staring at me like I've come from outer space.

There are obstacles everywhere to hearing. And this affects how I hear my son's world. I lament the idea of missing anything in his life because I can't hear it. Hearing is a critical aspect of how he connects to others, and I want only to connect with him, to hear the sounds that appeal to him, or the ones that frighten him. On our visit to a nature park, we joined a group hike, and near the end everyone gathered to listen for sounds in the woods. I heard nothing while everyone else listened. I watched my son's reactions to those invisible sounds, his eyes lighting up in wonder, tuned in to the sounds of nature. He was happy, and I was glad for him that he can do these things. It helps me to appreciate his experiences.

Once when we visited the neighborhood pool, my son played a game with a friend, a kind of listening exercise. My son and his friend and the friend's mother played. I watched them all, secretly wishing that I could play too, that I could share in that kind of game with him without trouble. It pained me that I couldn't. As he's gotten older, my son has gradually learned and better understands that Daddy can't hear well. Sometimes he remembers this, but most often he still forgets. It makes for difficult, awkward, or even funny conversations between us. I continue to give him gentle reminders, sometimes less gentle when I'm frustrated. Barriers in hearing have always existed for me with my disability. I've grappled with them in one way or another. As a parent, I feel a certain requirement to listen to my son's world more carefully with the expectation that I'm his advocate, that I'll protect him.

While it wounds me that I won't ever really hear my son's world the same way that he hears it, I want him to enjoy his life happily and free from any worry. I'll go on watching him as he hears and learns and grows, despite how fleeting the time is, despite the worries I have for him and for me. I think I'm lucky to be his father and to witness the small and large moments with him, to see him embrace the world in his own way. No matter the limitations to my hearing, I'll be able to see my son changing into the beautiful individual he is, and I'll be close by, ready to listen.

THREE DAYS BEFORE THE WITCHES FLY

SUZANNE NIELSEN

Since my adoptive mother's passing in 1993, I think of her like clockwork, each year on her birthday in October, three days before the witches fly. Her matriarchal voice bellows from the heavens the morning of, and she's shaking her finger insisting I must adhere to the female tribe now as the elder; the corners of her mouth form a smile, and her eyes look smaller, but still attentive. She hands me a note that validates my motherhood. She signs it, "Love, Mother." She closes her tiny eyes and talks as though in a trance, her eyes in perpetual motion under closed lids. She talks about how she was unavailable as a mother due to her dependency on tranquilizers, and how "no one hands you a book, a step-by-step manual for raising a child free of sorrow." She tells me this because she's been watching my progression through single parenthood, through dependency, through bouts of unyielding depression, and she's high-fiving me, blowing me kisses. I feel them touch my cheeks, and I widen my eyes. I hug myself and thank her for visiting me. I thank her for mothering me the only way she knew how. I blow kisses back. "I love you," I say. Three simple syllables that echo my heart.

I am an adoptee. I am a depressive. These things make up a part of who I am. They are my strengths and my challenges. I am also a mother. A mother to little me and big me; a mother to two adult sons, and it's the biggest privilege I've had in life.

If I listen closely, I sometimes hear echoes from the past. I recall the scene with Dad snoring in the recliner; Mom is outside watering flowers; siblings and half-siblings are yelling in unison, "Mom, watch me. Mom, did you see?" She watches them turn somersaults, stand on their heads, while eagerly awaiting her approval. Aunties are arguing in the kitchen; the uncles are quietly smoking in the living room watching *Wild Kingdom*. A pair of cousins are playing ping-pong in the basement. My mother asks me to go call my brother and cousin for supper. I open the door and yell the names of my three previous siblings. I close the door, and my mother kneels down to my height and says, "It's okay, Suzanne. Now go call your brother and cousin." I do so with vivid and murky memories competing until I sit down at the table and listen to the matriarchs pray to the heavens for nourishment.

My adoptive parents took me into their home shortly after I turned three. By age five, they had legally adopted me. Some memories I have from the transition seem vague, but others are vividly clear. I remember being in a room that echoed while people paced with tablets and pens, ignoring the huge smeared window behind the desk where a man sat in a black robe, glasses perched atop his head. Also in the chambers were my new mom and dad, along with a state-assigned social worker, and four talking heads whispering sentence fragments in the judge's ear. When we entered the room, my father tenderly lifted me onto the judge's desk, and there I sat while they mumbled about things I didn't understand. At some point, the judge looked at me, an elderly man whose thick glasses slid off his shiny head, and he asked, "You don't talk much, do you?" Somehow, I internalized this not as a question, but as a means of identification. I answered back immediately. "I do too talk." And yet I believe that specific moment triggered my many years of long bouts of silence.

I invite you into the courtroom, sixty years later, primarily to give you a glimpse into markers of the moments when shame, vulnerability, abandonment, and an overwhelming feeling of being odd claimed its space in my psyche. Years later these markers would be identified, according to the *Diagnostic and Statistical Manual of Mental Disorders* (DSM-5), as clinical depression. With therapy, I learned to provoke the silence within. I learned that I needed to identify with my psyche. I needed to comprehend what harbored within, and to accept my challenge, my depression. I needed to learn to not be afraid of it, to not be ashamed of it. I needed to understand how my mother's dependency transformed her invisible depression into a world of silence. My mother could not admit that depression ruled the roost for so many of my developing years. My mother could not admit to her own preexisting depression. Although the two of us butted heads infinitely, we agreed to disagree about whether depression was at the root of the problem.

The instinctual defiance, and the shame that elapsed in that courtroom sixty years ago, was my first conscious awareness that I was, in fact, inferior. When feeling inferior, you find your own devices to shield you. These become instinctual to ward off predators. To this day I have the physical motion of rocking. I am rocking to my own rhythm as I write this. I am sitting in a straight-backed chair, and I am rocking. I find this motion comforting and instinctual. I don't realize that I am moving in the slightest. I routinely rock myself to sleep. Many childhood afternoons, I craved my white rocking chair inside my private bedroom, staring out the window at the overgrown weeping willow, where I played house, which, upon reflection, was a strange form of play: I'd be inside the house, usually alone and content, envisioning my pre-birth existence, my embryonic goo forming and floating, reacting to the sounds sent through an umbilical connection.

For the past four decades, I've lived with swallowing antidepressants, and overall, this keeps me functioning fairly steadily, with some side effects. In addition to working with a psychiatrist, I've worked with neurologists, psychologists, acupuncturists, chiropractors, physical trainers, and psychics. I've tried biofeedback, talk therapy, exercise, needles, an array of antidepressants, meditation, MariEl healing (a form of hands-on healing that teaches you to mother the child within), prescription drugs, street drugs, alcohol, and sobriety—I'll stop there. The modes of therapies occasionally complement one another, sometimes contradict one another. But for a long time, and still occasionally, I feel like the gerbil on the wheel, the dog chasing its tail, the polar bear pacing at Como Zoo.

In the basement is where my youngest son paces. He isolates with chemical dependency and depression, unwilling to address the depression via medication. He and I talk at times into the early hours about ways to escape its claws. He's completed a thirty-day drug treatment program, and a four-month residential aftercare program. He's kind and intuitive, and he recognizes his challenges. Over a three-year period, Evan and I became familiar with juvenile court, and his last courtroom appearance brought me back to the judge's chamber, where I sat scared and voiceless so many years previous. I looked at my child, the one who wears his feelings on his face, sitting scared and voiceless.

"That is a fact, Evan. They do seem to survive." We sat there listening to the modes of movement. The boat motors roared, the seagulls squeaked. The sky was almost one consistent shade of blue. "I could stay here forever," Evan said. Then it dawned on me; there was a rhythm that soothed him. I watched as he tapped his right foot to what was swaying him, a habit he'd developed before he set foot in school. The angst was moving into his foot and burying itself deep within the warmth of the sand. "We can stay here as long as you like," I said. I grabbed his hand and squeezed it three times while I rocked back and forth so naturally. Three squeezes mean I Love You, if you count the syllables.

IT MUST BE IN OUR GENES

KAZ MORRAN

"You're not serious, are you?" said Dr. Newman.

I held out the one-way ticket to Tokyo I'd just spent my life savings on.

He waved it aside and turned up his nose. "You can't get the same treatment over there."

"I can't get the same opportunities here."

"You're being irresponsible. Do you have any idea how hard it's going to be to find a specialist?" Dr. Newman leaned forward across his desk, making sure to lock eyes so the point got through to my little twenty-four-year-old brain. "Twenty to twenty-four percent of people with northern European ancestry"—that meant me—"carry the HLA-B27 gene. Of those, only around two percent develop the joint and spine problems associated with ankylosing spondylitis. In Japan, that number is less than half of one percent."

"I know," I said.

Dr. Newman threw up his hands. "Well, good luck finding a specialist for a disease nobody has."

* * *

Evan and I drove home that midmorning in silence as the echoes from that room bounced off the dashboard of the car. I replayed the verdict over and over in my head. The court had ordered Evan to complete an in-patient treatment program once again. It was October 2007, and the witches would be flying later in the month. My mother's birthday would come and go. Evan would extend his stay in aftercare, and I saw him fight like a tiger to break free from depression's hold. I think back to the tribe: Aunt Lil, Esther, my grandmother. I think of the men in my family mesmerized by *Wild Kingdom*.

If only a child came with an instruction manual. No one prepares you for the depths of motherhood. Perhaps Evan will take life a day at a time; maybe meds might be considered. Over time the highs and lows of my depression have become more regulated, and this allows me to live life, not just survive life. Medication for my invisible disease seems to keep me on track. It tames the tiger within but doesn't extinguish the fight. I still hear echoes of insecurity, but I no longer run from them. In a strange way, the echoes that used to haunt me now are warning signs to keep going. Move through the fog, surrender to yourself long enough to hear the noise, and mother the child within.

I think of my life before medication, fourteen years of age, when I felt hopeless and stupid. I ran without a destination like a wild tiger, no camouflage, no voice, no contribution to society. At sixty-three, I've groomed the rhythm that soothes me, my way to mother myself, my attempt to pass for normal. In my quiet time, I sometimes call upon the matriarchs to gently push me forward.

They've set an example for me to contribute to society, and I watch as my sons contribute to society. My eldest, Commander Major Murphy, is finishing up a three-year assignment with

Special Forces Underwater Operations School in Key West. He serves our country with a passion and honor that brings tears to my eyes. Silent and stoic, he holds his feelings close to his heart like his body armor. He finished an Ironman Triathlon with a broken collar bone. He is disciplined like many first children are. I just spent a week with him in the Keys, and although we didn't talk much, I noticed the lines surrounding his eyes, and I think of what he's seen in Afghanistan and many other places of war-torn destruction; I think of the adrenaline rush he must have experienced seeing his blood pour out of a gunshot wound. There's a tiger within, tamed and controlled. This was my first trip since COVID.

In March of 2020, the year of COVID-19, I traveled to Tarpon Springs, Florida, where Evan had relocated a year earlier. On the drive from the airport to Evan's apartment, I rattled on about the imposition of the virus's strange and surreal reality. Evan took a detour; we parked the car and walked a hundred feet to the water. "This is my favorite place to come and sit," Evan said. We sat next to the Gulf's gentle tide and let the midafternoon sun warm our bottoms. We stared into the vastness of the ocean in front of us. I asked Evan how he was doing. He lit a joint and said, "You know, Mom, up and down." He stared ahead and spotted a manatee, and then another. "The males always follow the females," he said. They were huge and carefree. "That's smart of them to do so," I replied. Evan laughed and said, "They're matriarchs, I guess."

I thought on that while I watched them float, almost lifeless.

"Do you think they're depressed? Their bodies get so beat up here by boat motors. I watch them a lot and their scars are pretty deep, but they survive," Evan said.

It Must Be in Our Genes

I was eleven when my mom moved us to the Okanagan Valley in British Columbia, where the warm, dry climate—a rarity in Canada—and access to specialists would make life a little kinder to her recently diagnosed firstborn. Unfortunately, the new town offered little for Mom. Unable to find work, and raising two boys on her own, she somehow managed to make sure we never missed a meal. Adapting, I learned, was just something people did.

If Mom had a good reason for leaving my dad, I'd never heard it. And from Dad, I only had memories of him complaining about his back. So, I vowed two things: to never moan about pain and to never pass on the HLA-B27 gene.

* * *

The disease and I grew together, changing, evolving, adapting. At sixteen, when the jolts from skates hitting ice became too much for my spine, I switched from forward to goalie. Later, when the only jobs available were hard labor, or the climate proved too harsh for my joints, I moved, hitching from town to town. I lived in ten homes in five years, including a stint with no home at all.

Willpower alone might've kept me afloat, if not for a drunken midnight slide down a snowy hill. Neither the ER doctor nor my new boss would take me seriously. "You wouldn't be walking if you broke it," they both said. Four workdays later, I returned to the hospital and found the X-rays said otherwise. A Y-shaped fracture had split the middlemost vertebrae—permanently, it had turned out.

"You got Tylenol at home?" said the doctor.

"Yeah, but I had to take half the bottle to walk here and can't get more till payday."

It's not true, in my experience, about time or laughter being the best healers. For spinal fractures, morphine works better. But the doctor did not agree, and he refused to prescribe anything on top of my regular meds.

* * *

When my fiancée got pregnant, our emotions swayed wildly. I saw no way to afford a baby, but the real fear came from HLA-B27. And yet, when she confessed her own trepidation came from uncertainty over who the father was, a part of me wondered if playing dad to someone else's baby wouldn't be my only chance to raise a healthy child. Not that it'd matter: my fiancée went and had an abortion against my wishes, and a week later, downed a bottle of my pills. Her reasons were stacked upon one another, and all had come crashing down at once—depression, bipolar disorder, drug and alcohol abuse, the stress of poverty. But heaviest of all had been the guilt and shame.

* * *

It's funny sometimes how things unfold if you let them. To others, I must have looked quite lost and derelict: a twenty-three-year-old drifter, limping and hunched beneath the weight of the little backpack that held my only possessions. While true that I had no definite destination or even a map, I had two thumbs that worked just fine to help me bounce top to bottom, coast to coast around the continent. After 8,000 miles, I'd discovered far too much to ever feel lost.

During beers after work with the regulars, one biker asked what I'd do once the kitchen shut down for the winter. Shut down? That was news to me.

The music changed from "Hotel California" to "Highway to Hell," and the biker asked if I knew AC/DC was Australian. He added, "You know, winter here is their summer."

* * *

By the ninth month of my year Down Under, with the tropical heat, the town- and job-hopping, long hours standing in a kitchen, the inadequate medication, the drinking—my body grounded me in Perth, a city with a Californian climate, the "Hell" where AC/DC's "Highway" goes, and a good place to ride out the remaining three months of my visa.

If the pain itself wasn't enough to signal the need for a career change, a look in the mirror at the beginnings of a hunchback was. But what work could a poorly educated cripple do? The answer came from my new friends. A large portion of the backpackers in Perth are Japanese, and of the many I hung out with, one young woman caught my eye.

"Can you teach me this word?" Natsumi asked, showing me the spy novel in her hand.

"Which one?"

"Umm..." She smiled shyly. "Everything. I don't understand everything."

With my visa up, Natsumi and I parted in the same way so many intercultural backpacker romances end: with a promise to meet again.

*   *   *

Although prescriptions are optional in some parts of the world, finding meds that approximate what you'd get back home can be a choose-your-own-adventure; however, in my experience, this does not mean pharmacists act carelessly. A pharmacist in Bangkok went to great lengths to bridge the language barrier and understand my condition. It's no exaggeration to say she changed my life by introducing me to my first wonder drug, Tramacet.

My delight at having easily and cheaply acquired an ungodly supply of the painkiller gave me cause for reflection. For the first time since childhood, and despite the oppressive tropical humidity, I felt liberated. Lighter. Nimble. I could walk down the street without wincing in pain. I could unclench the jaw I hadn't realized I'd been clenching. I was surely taking way more than the recommended dose. My back and joints still hurt, of course, but the pain had been knocked down several levels—enough that I gained the courage to invite Natsumi to come join me for a month-long holiday along the Mekong through Thailand, Cambodia, Laos, and Vietnam.

It must have been love, because the trip sealed our relationship, despite our ideas of a "holiday" turning out to be as different as our upbringings. I was perfectly happy, through the aid of my new meds, to cram inside a seatless, un-air-conditioned minivan with thirty strangers (some touted AK-47s or live chickens; some rode on the roof) for eighteen hours of land-mined cliffhanging dirt roads. Natsumi, however, whose biggest adversity till then had been college exams, was less content. Even still, by the end of the trip, we had our sights set on a life together in Japan.

* * *

A couple hundred miles north of Tokyo is Sendai (population one million), a place known for its samurai past and mild climate. Mild compared to the humidity farther south and the bitter cold farther north, anyway.

Natsumi wouldn't move from her hometown to Sendai for another half-year. Until I could show her and—more importantly—her parents that she'd have a better life away from home with a strange foreigner, I was on my own. In Japan, companies only hire in April, and I'd come in September. "Come back in a year when you can speak better Japanese," the job office told me. My visa stipulated I had to secure work and an address within three months or go home. Nobody would rent to me either ("Sorry, no foreigners"), so, with my savings dropping fast, I stayed at a youth hostel. I hit up every English school in town, breaking the bank on a bicycle to get around more efficiently, but not only were my cold calls unappreciated, I learned my teaching certificate meant little without a university degree.

But I got lucky.

A little Canadian flag in a downtown window caught my eye. Turned out, the owner of a one-room English school for kids and adults had just fired her only teacher, a Canadian, for missing lessons due to a diabetes-induced hospitalization.

"The students like Canadians," Goto-san said. "If you can pass a trial lesson, I'll start you right away."

I readily agreed, and, to my surprise, she immediately brought in six adult students and told me, "The lesson isn't scheduled to start for ten more minutes, so you have time to prepare. There's a shelf of textbooks behind you. Their level is around TOEIC 400, but they're weak with participles and relative clauses."

Eh? I nodded as if it all made perfect sense. "I'm good to start anytime if everyone else is ready," I heard myself say. Idiot.

I'd never done any kind of public speaking before, and the prospect of teaching a group while someone stood by with a clipboard terrified me. But I must've done okay. I got the job, though Goto-san questioned why I hadn't used the whiteboard or textbooks.

"Since this was my first time with these particular students, I thought I'd keep things conversational to gauge their individual requirements."

PT Barnum would've been impressed, as was Goto-san. "Adaptable. Improvisational," she mused.

The next day, a photographer came in and had me pose for a portrait to be used for PR, including on billboards. "Sit up straight," Goto-san, her assistant, a photographer, and the photographer's assistant kept demanding. They even grabbed my shoulders to force my spine to conform. I strained against the tension in my back so as not to let the shards of pain wreck my smile.

Goto-san had me see a doctor of her choosing for a medical letter stating I was fit to work. This turned out to be a blessing in disguise since my meds from Canada were almost out. I was open with the doctor about my ankylosing spondylitis, and in the letter to Goto-san, he simply wrote "Back stiffness due to sports injury" and that it wouldn't affect my work. He happily prescribed equivalents of my regular meds, including Tramacet, albeit at a much lower dose.

The biggest challenge—teaching children—came a few days later, and every Thursday thereafter for two and a half years at an elementary school in a nearby coastal town. The twelve-hour day began in the gym, where I sang and danced and generally acted like a fool in front of three hundred preschoolers. The task repeated with kindergarteners, then first graders, followed by lessons in each individual classroom, second through seventh grade. I cherished every one of those kids and still remember many of their faces and names. It did not miss Natsumi that every Thursday I'd return home exhausted but feeling fulfilled. It can get tiresome, being a foreigner in Japan. No one ever asks your name, only where you're from and when you're going "home." Children, however, get over that othering instinct quickly. Was that why I liked being around the kids? Or was there something more?

"Have you thought about us having children?" Natsumi asked.

A slow smile crept from the corners of my mouth, only to be snatched away by the thought of HLA-B27.

* * *

A week after Natsumi and I got engaged in March of 2008, Goto-san presented me with a congratulatory gift and news that as of April 1, I'd be unemployed. "We usually only keep our teacher for a year, but you did such a good job with the kids ... I'm sure they're going to miss you."

I was devastated. Japan loves its suit-and-tie ceremonies, and I'd been there alongside weeping parents for the most important events in these children's lives: annual commencements and graduations, pageants and recitals, and sports days. I'd admired their artwork on the walls, bandaged their scraped knees, and consoled them from bullies.

Though unintended, the message was as clear as it was harsh: They aren't your children. If you want kids, have your own.

***

January 1, 2009, we got married in Cancún, bought a fixer-upper in the suburbs of Sendai, and got a dog. ESL work was plentiful if not stable, freelance-teaching at one venue or another. Only one thing was missing. Natsumi was first to bring up the subject of children, so I knew she favored the idea. I had concerns. But Natsumi put me at ease.

"It would be your job to teach him or her how to deal with it," she said of the chance of me passing on the HLA gene.

Oddly, the thought of such a responsibility was what converted me. The more I mulled it over, the more I pictured myself as a father. And besides, the chance of our child inheriting the disease was relatively low.

"Okay," I said. "Let's have a baby."

But first: disaster.

***

At a magnitude of 9.1, the six-minute quake of March 11, 2011, was among the strongest ever recorded—powerful enough to shift the Earth's axis ten inches, permanently slowing the planet's rotation and shortening the length of a day by 1.8 microseconds. Sendai was about as close to the epicenter as you could get and got slammed by a 133-foot, 435-mile-per-hour tsunami. The waves reached six miles inland. Fortunately, our home is twelve miles from shore and just outside the evacuation radius of the Fukushima nuclear meltdown.

As a result of this massive disaster, 19,500 people died, many of them at washed-away evacuation centers. I've decided it's best not to inquire about how the elementary school I used to teach at fared.

It would be months before an entire hour passed without an aftershock and a year until we had a tremor-free day or night. Officially, there were 869 aftershocks measuring greater than 5.0, 118 of which were over 6.0. The disaster was like nothing I'd been through or could have imagined, but—I hesitate to proclaim—it really was no big deal for me personally. I feel guilty saying that, given how badly others suffered. Close to a decade later, there are still highway exit signs where the names of entire towns have been painted over. Hundreds of miles of coastline remain a washout.

In the aftermath, our neighborhood went without electricity for a week and running water for three. It took months to get back gas for cooking and hot showers or gasoline to drive. In that first week, Natsumi and I snuggled up to keep warm. We rationed the pantry, emptied the freezer onto the barbecue, gathered with neighbors in the park to boil rice on an open fire, and waited for hours in the snow for water from army trucks or at the supermarket for what paltry snacks remained. And through it all, my back, knees, hips, neck, and legs ached like they've never ached before. It all piled up: standing in the cold, damp air, trying to make my meds last, and sleeping downstairs on the hardwood, unsure if the next aftershock would collapse the second floor.

And yet, I never had a moment when I thought we couldn't handle it. I never felt anxious or overwhelmed. The days were certainly somber, especially as news poured in of the extent of the devastation, but Natsumi and I were nowhere close to being in a life-threatening situation. I don't consider us "survivors." People who had to cling to the floating fragments of their roof for three days were survivors. Not us. We were merely inconvenienced. We had to make some adjustments, but that's what people do in life. They adapt.

To Natsumi, however, this was nothing less than the pinnacle of suffering and the prelude to the apocalypse.

"What if the house collapses?" she repeatedly asked.

I bundled myself in makeshift radiation wear and went out and inspected the foundation and support columns. "It won't. The cracks are minor."

"But what if does?"

"Then we'll get an apartment."

"What if we don't have jobs to go back to?"

"We'll find new ones."

"And if the radiation blows into Sendai?"

"We'll go somewhere else."

"But the roads are closed. There's no gas. The airport's underwater!"

"If we have to, we'll walk to your parents' place."

"Walk? That's two hundred miles! Are you insane?"

"We wouldn't do it all in one day."

"What if we run out of water?"

"There's a creek. And snow higher up."

"And food?"

"Plenty of pigeons."

She didn't laugh. I knew we'd be fine, because we'd do what we had to do to make sure we were fine. Natsumi fell into depression. I wanted to get out, go for walks, get the yard ready for spring. After all, when else would we have so much free time? But she could only stay in and cry at the TV.

I got called back to work the second the power came back on—two weeks before I'd get a hot shower. Natsumi, too.

"Already?" I asked my boss over the phone.

"Yes. The Japanese staff has been here cleaning the place up since the day after the earthquake."

"Have the city inspectors cleared it to reopen?" I spoke.

My boss replied, "If you can't make it in, we'll have to find someone who will."

To avoid inflicting Natsumi with the additional stress of an unemployed husband, I did as my boss said, but my apparent insolence got me knocked down to part-time. No matter. I set my sights on grander pursuits.

Truth be told, I'd been two credits short of receiving a high school diploma. I'd never lied, but no one had asked. I quickly got a GED, then spent a year taking online courses—math and engineering, astrophysics, and astronomy—in a bid to enroll in the aerospace engineering program at nearby Tohoku University, the highest-ranked in the country.

My application was promptly denied.

Yet, a new sort of adaptation had been seeded: if I couldn't be a rocket scientist, maybe I could write science fiction. But that, too, would have to wait.

Natsumi was pregnant.

* * *

We named our son Taiyo. It means "the sun," the giver of warmth and light, the brightest star in the sky, and he's the center of our solar system. Shortly after his birth, I got an offer to teach English and give lectures to engineering students at Tohoku University, a nice supplement to the freelance lessons.

Taiyo's eight now. We haven't had him tested for the HLA gene, and symptoms wouldn't appear until he's at least ten, anyway. It's not understood what environmental triggers make the disease manifest, but given how low ankylosing spondylitis rates are among Japanese, I'm hopeful about his odds. He just finished second grade, top of the class. Quick-witted and creative. Happy, active, and very healthy. He plays hockey, is fluent in both Japanese and English, and wants to be an astronaut or paleontologist, or, somehow, a combination of the two.

We go on adventures. Natsumi thinks we're nuts, so she stays home, and we head out whichever way the wind blows. Already, Taiyo's been to eleven countries. He's hiked up smoldering volcanoes, through steamy jungles, and over great desert dunes; he's crammed into subway cars, street markets, and elevators in the world's tallest buildings; ridden bamboo rafts, maglev trains, and scooters through the Global South's traffic; held bugs the size of his forearm, fed crocodiles in the wild, and had a mooing contest with water buffalo in a rice paddy. We've stayed in some pretty suspect hotels and faced off against some questionable cuisine, but the only time he complains is when it's time to go home.

Never once has Tai shown impatience when I can't keep up or must sit an activity out. He motivates me to stay in shape, and my second wonder drug makes it easier—a TNF inhibitor I self-inject twice a month. There's still pain, and I still need the other meds, but there's no more having to psych myself up just to get out of bed.

*　*　*

I go upstairs. I'm tired and sore from skating, but the sound of Taiyo's snoring puts a smile on my face. Two instances of broken arms have driven me to finally quit hockey.

"Next time could be your neck," Natsumi had said. "Is it worth the risk of not being able to play with your son?"

I agreed, but, of course, I never really quit. I just changed my role. These days, I help coach Taiyo's team, teaching kids to skate and shoot the puck—or stop it, in Taiyo's case.

There's an earthquake. I stand in the doorway of Taiyo's room. Though the windows rattle around him, the soft streetlight coming in through the shoji paper screen doesn't change. It's the biggest quake in about a year: 7.4, I'll later learn. The mounds of Lego on the floor jangle, and I reach down to put a finger on the tip of his creation—a rocket—so it doesn't fall. At the peak of the shaking, Tai's eyes flutter open. He lifts his head and mutters, "Cool," upon seeing the glowing ceiling stars in a frenzy. "I can feel the plates in the Earth moving." He yawns and returns to snoring. I sit for a minute on the edge of his bed and rub the back of my neck.

It's already humid and not yet rainy season.

I think about what's next for us. Here we are, April 2020, surrounded by a threat we cannot see but hear about every day on the news. School is closed. Classes cancelled. Both Natusmi and I have lost our jobs. But it's fine. Work opportunities in Japan had been drying up anyway. This is merely the breeze to clean the dust off the slate.

I've been preparing for this all my life.

Here I am, writing this, waiting for the barbecue to warm up, and in the middle of writing my second novel. A new career awaits, but not here. Not in Japan. We've decided to move to Canada.

* * *

Whether or not Taiyo ends up with ankylosing spondylitis, I must make sure he's ready for whatever life throws at him. Adaptability is a skill I want him to develop without having to go through the same hardships that I have, but adaptability grows out of overcoming adversity, and life in Japan tends toward rigid uniformity—not a lot of variation in a child's path. We're not very wealthy but will always have what we need. The lack of a daily struggle in Taiyo's life (beyond the stress of an exam) used to worry me. Now I realize that no matter who or where you are, life always finds something to chuck at you.

* * *

Taiyo comes home from the park, not in tears but upset. He's been bullied for being different. For being a "half-breed."

"Don't worry," I tell him. "You'll work it out."

"How do you know?"

"You always do."

"I do?"

"Sure," I say. "We both do."

"We do?"

"Remember in Vietnam when we got stuck out in the rain on the motorbike?"

He laughs. "Yeah."

"And what'd we do?"

"We took off our wet socks and made them into one big soggy ball and we played soccer in the rain for like an hour while we waited for the rain to stop, but it didn't stop."

"And then?"

"And then we drove back to the hotel even though it was still raining super hard."

"And then?"

"And then we put on new socks and went to the night market and ate bugs."

"Exactly."

He laughs so hard he has to grab his tummy. "I guess maybe we are kind of good at making things work out," he says. "How come?"

"It must be in our genes."

ACKNOWLEDGMENTS

We are grateful to everyone everywhere fighting for disability justice.

Our thanks to everyone who supported and believed in Pen 2 Paper, especially our volunteer judges, donors, and the staff at CTD. Thanks to Heidi Johnson-Wright for getting this whole anthology project started, and to Belo Cipriani for making the dream come true. Thank you to the contributors for trusting us with your work.

Thank you, Sandy White. Thank you, Juan and Geoff.

ABOUT THE EDITORS

SUSIE ANGEL & LAURA PERNA

A Dallas native, Laura received her bachelor's in English from the University of Texas at Austin and her master's in Italian literature from New York University.

Gloria "Susie" Angel was raised in Boston and California before moving to Austin, Texas, in 1987, where she earned an associate's degree in communications from Austin Community College and a bachelor's in magazine journalism from the University of Texas at Austin.

Laura and Susie began their adventures together as volunteers, then staff, at the Coalition of Texans with Disabilities, where they co-coordinated Pen 2 Paper, a disability-focused creative writing competition; wrote newsletters and member communications; advocated for a number of disability issues to the state legislature; supported events; started a monthly inclusive open mic; grumbled a lot; envisioned a better world; became friends; became family.

A TRIBUTE TO SUSIE

On August 20, 2022, the Coalition of Texans with Disabilities family said goodbye to our colleague and friend, Gloria Susan Angel, or, as everyone knew her, Susie.

At CTD, Susie and I often found ourselves working together, most notably on Pen 2 Paper (more on that in this book's foreword). What we did with Pen 2 Paper, though imperfect, remains some of the most meaningful work I've ever been a part of, and I'll be delighted and deeply humbled to the end of my days that I got to do it with her.

Collaborating with Oleb Books and the wonderful authors included in this anthology meant the world to Susie. An advocate and artist herself, she got a lot of joy and sense of purpose from lifting up the work of other disabled writers. She continued doggedly to plug away on this collection, even as her health declined. The foreword to this book is the last major project she worked on.

In all areas of her work at CTD, Susie took every assignment and task to heart, taking care to produce the best work possible. It's safe to say that she would have approached any position with the same dedication. But with us, she was often advocating for policy and cultural changes that would have affected her own life, as a person with a disability. The last pieces of legislation she worked on have expanded access to healthcare and protected voting rights for Texans with disabilities.

Susie also took every opportunity to advocate for a raise in the wage of community attendants. She knew firsthand how difficult it is to find help at a subpoverty wage rate of $8.11 per hour. Her own attendant and close friend of many years, Sandy White, a quiet woman with an endless capacity for love and care, passed away unexpectedly a couple months before Susie's health declined. It is not difficult to connect the dots here, adding another layer of despair, as well as frustration and anger, to our grief.

But to speak about Susie only in terms of sadness and anger would be in error. She was a person who sought—and often found or created—joy, meaning, and community. In the office, with her congregation at the Austin New Church, in the mixed-ability dance group Body Shift, at the Lion & Pirate open mic (which she helped to get off the ground and continued to support through 2022), at any ballpark (particularly, Dell Diamond), or wherever she found herself, Susie was quick to make a friend and have a good time. Even in her final weeks, when she was uncomfortable and immensely frustrated with her care, she managed to crack a joke and a smile when any of her friends and family would visit her.

Susie hated it when people told her that God would heal her disabilities. She believed God made her exactly as she was, on purpose, because she was uniquely suited to the task of showing how people with disabilities were as capable and human as anyone else, of leading by example. In this, she excelled. I take some measure of comfort knowing that her work in this regard remains in effect, and will continue for many years, through all of the people, legislation, and creative work she touched, including this volume.

www.ingramcontent.com/pod-product-compliance
Lightning Source LLC
Chambersburg PA
CBHW030555080526
44585CB00012B/381